One Voice

One Voice
Using Music and Stories in the Classroom

BARBARA M. BRITSCH

AMY DENNISON-TANSEY

Illustrated by
MELANIE FINDLING

1995
TEACHER IDEAS PRESS
A Division of
Libraries Unlimited, Inc.
Englewood, Colorado

To all the Arts Unlimited children and teachers, for inviting me inside their stories.—BB

To my husband Brian and my daughter Eira, for their support and patience during the preparation of this book. I am forever grateful.—AD-T

TEACHER IDEAS PRESS
A Division of Libraries Unlimited, Inc.
P.O. Box 6633
Englewood, CO 80155-6633
1-800-237-6124

Production Editor: Jason Cook
Copy Editor: Ramona Gault
Typesetting and Interior Design: Kay Minnis

Library of Congress Cataloging-in-Publication Data

Britsch, Barbara Martin.
    One voice : using music and stories in the classroom / Barbara M. Britsch, Amy Dennison-Tansey ; illustrated by Melanie Findling.
    xxiv, 175 p. 22x28 cm.
    Includes bibliographical references and index.
    ISBN 1-56308-049-4
    1. School music--Instruction and study. 2. Storytelling. 3. Music in education. 4. Elementary school teaching. I. Dennison-Tansey, Amy. II. Title.
    MT930.B83   1995
    372.87--dc20   95-11838
                                                                        CIP
                                                                        MN
                                                                        Rev.

Contents

PART II

Preface

Music and narrative have an ancient and close relationship. The bard sang of heroic deeds and exploits of rulers and leaders; the wandering griot of Africa still sings the news from village to village; today's folksingers comment on the concerns of society. The blending of these two art forms comes naturally to us from our experiences as the performing music and storytelling duo WordWinds and as teachers of music and storytelling at the Toledo Museum of Art. We discovered through our work that combining music and stories greatly enriches and enhances the essence of each art. Meaning, mood, form, even the color of music and stories are heightened through this synthesis.

This book is intended to offer teachers a practical and theoretical classroom guide to the many ways music and stories may be explored, both independently and in tandem, to give students a better understanding and appreciation of each art form separately and of their power together. The activities have been tested on students and developed with the general classroom teacher in mind.

This material is not meant to be the definitive answer to teaching storytelling, literature, or music. There are fine books for children and adults that detail these processes. We have tried to choose activities that are complete in themselves for each art form, that parallel each other, and that may be fused to enable students to experience the processes common to both music and stories: listening (reflecting and analyzing), composing (creating), and performing (doing).

The crucial aspect of all these activities is original productions by students. Improvisational music and drama, *child*-centered art, and *child*-created story orchestrations, for instance, will empower students to experience the imaginative possibilities of music and storytelling.

The primary audience for this book is classroom teachers, generally kindergarten through sixth grade, as well as music specialists. Storytellers also will find suggestions for enhancing stories with music, as will teachers or leaders in settings such as day-care centers, camps, and museums.

Michael Moore, in a speech entitled "A Tale of Two Paradigms" (given in June 1992 at Bowling Green State University, Ohio) offered a rationale for the importance of the arts:

> Aesthetic education gives us access to new ways of communication and thinking, by unlocking some of the most powerful tools of learning that lie within each of us. It offers freedom because it celebrates the uniqueness of each human being while at the same time it reaffirms our membership in the family of the world.

We invite you to take your own journey through the world of music and stories, mapping the way for students, discovering your own story to sing. We encourage *you* to chart the expedition for students. Use this book as a tour guide, to define a destination, to discover and enlighten the stops on the class journey. Our concluding hope is that you and your students will discover the fundamental reality of the world of music and stories.

Acknowledgments

Special thanks to Melanie, for her lighthearted, childlike artwork, and for her patience. To Suzanne Barchers, for her enthusiasm and encouragement as we began this project. To Barbara Coleman, for her insight and good-natured willingness to critique activities. To Dr. Michael Moore, for permission to quote him as "philosopher-in-residence." To Pam, for unfailingly appropriate suggestions. To Roger, for cheers and support. To all the teachers and students we have performed for and worked with over the years. To all our listeners, for listening. To the Mattel Company. To our editor, Jason Cook, for help and understanding.

Introduction

USING THIS BOOK EFFECTIVELY

A map, a compass, traveler's checks, a flashlight, keys, appropriate clothes, rain gear—proper equipment for a journey. Just so, this introduction will equip you for a journey into stories and music.

Included in this book are suggested stories and musical selections that work well with the activities, extensive music and story bibliographies, and chapters that demonstrate how to make simple musical instruments and how to experiment with various bookbinding techniques. Part I, chapters 1 through 4, moves from a general response to stories and music to students and teachers exploring the inner world of these art forms. Each chapter begins with an introduction to the chapter's theme, followed by a series of story activities generally arranged by age and complexity. Next are musical activities in the same arrangement. These chapters each culminate with a group of collaborative activities that integrate stories and music. Part II, chapters 5 and 6, contains instructions on making instruments and books in the classroom as an integral part of this journey. Concluding this book are a general bibliography; a bibliography of books about music, making instruments, and making books; a discography; a list of sources for instruments, books, and recordings; and a glossary of literary elements, literary terms, and music terms.

Activities in this book

- provide concepts and ways to explore those concepts;

- are not "make-it-take-it" activities, but focus on process;

- serve as a model for your own selection and choice of material;

- can be used out of sequence;

- include basic thinking skills of problem-solving, patterning, classifying, interpreting, predicting, observing, and reflecting;

- are recommended for certain ages but can certainly be adapted to other ages, levels, and abilities; and

- challenge students to use creative thinking skills and imagination.

STORYTELLING IN THE CLASSROOM

Defining Story

The word *stories* in the title of this book refers both to the folktales and authored books suggested in the activities and listed in appendix A, and to the idea of "story" as a paradigm for narrative fiction as an art form, from a simple short story to a lengthy novel. We hope that, as you and your students engage in these activities, your responses to the stories will be full of delight and wonder, and that you will begin to discover how story elements work together to form a work of art. The folktales referred to in the activities are, like all folklore, almost entirely "plot," that is, action with little description and undeveloped characters. The activities, however, suggest "walking around inside stories" to discover a great deal more about the characters and the settings, a perfectly legitimate exercise.

For the folktales and stories presented herein, we have chosen to emphasize four literary elements: plot, character, setting, and theme. There are other elements, such as point of view, style, and tone, but the basic four form a structure appropriate for this book.

> *Plot* is the series of events in a story: what happens and in what order. These events usually follow the familiar pattern of rising action, climactic event, and falling action (resolution). Plot also includes conflict. Opposing forces may be person against person, person against society, person against self, or person against nature. Many stories contain more than one conflict. Older students (age 10 and up) can be encouraged to recognize cause-and-effect relationships in a story's events as a basic story pattern.

> *Character*, as a literary element, suggests exploring the many facets of story characters: How and what do they think? Why do they behave as they do? What is their personality? What kind of clothing might they wear? What books would they like to read? And so on. Authors and tellers of folktales present characters through several devices. We come to know characters by what they say, by what others say about them, by their thoughts, and certainly by their behavior. Narrative description also helps; this is more common in authored stories than in folklore.

> *Setting* includes far more than the time and place of a story. The weather, for example, can be critical in a story's events. Heroes in folklore often find it necessary to confront powerful natural forces. A garden, a forest, the sea, for instance, can influence a character's course of action. The social or political climate of a story can tell us much about the culture the story comes from.

> *Theme* is the most elusive of the four elements, as, in well-written stories, it is seldom stated openly, except as a moral in fables and the occasional folktale. Theme can be simply defined as the central idea or ideas implied in a story, or, perhaps, the thoughts that remain with the reader. Worthwhile children's literature has themes of concern to children (and to all of us): friendship, honesty, courage, self-image, and family love, for example.

Many children enter school with a strong sense of story, knowing that a story is written down in a book and that they can read or tell it over and over, and a sense that a story has a shape—a beginning, a middle, and an end. By exploring stories with students, their innate sense of story will be heightened, whether or not the literary elements per se are directly mentioned. Recognizing, developing, and using story patterns in their own writing will enhance students' experience of literature.

Most stories suggested in the activities are folktales, for several reasons. They are easy to find; there is a wealth of folktales in picture-storybook versions and in collections. Books listed in the references following each chapter and in appendixes A and B can be readily found in most libraries and bookstores. We have found, in school residencies, that children are not always as familiar as they should be with these enduring and appealing tales. Whatever our background, world folklore is part of our heritage. Folktales can be a source for learning about many cultures and countries. Have intermediate- and upper-level students read collections of tales from various countries (assign one collection to a small group) and make notes on specific characteristics or references in the stories to the following concepts:

- Value system—objects, behaviors, and beliefs that are held in esteem or rewarded
- Religious practices—expressions of beliefs concerning a deity or deities, formalized religious roles, institutions, and rituals
- Social organizations—the manner in which people or groups formally or informally relate to each other; social-class distinctions
- Family structure—the ways members of a family interrelate; defined roles; deference patterns
- Economic patterns—occupations; ways in which people use resources for personal, family, or social welfare
- Governmental mode—the ways in which people are formally governed in a country, village, tribe, or other designated structure; their roles and responsibilities

It is fascinating to discover how details of a culture are embedded in its folklore. Finally, and most important for the classroom, folktales are perfect for storytelling.

The Importance of Storytelling in Education

Although this book looks at stories in a broader, more literary context than storytelling, the effect of telling stories is so powerful, it is well worth consideration. All the story activities can be done nicely with reading. You do not have to be a storyteller to use this book effectively, and many of the following remarks apply equally to reading as to telling. Storytelling is not better than reading—it is simply a different way of presenting a story. Once you experience students' responses to storytelling, however, you may wish to make storytelling part of the curriculum, with both you and the children as tellers and listeners. Storytelling performances, festivals, and resident artists are other possibilities. Appendix A lists books that can serve as the groundwork for these activities.

Storytelling in the classroom is gaining recognition as a legitimate and appealing way of experiencing our literary and cultural heritages. Professional storytellers abound; researchers are increasingly engaging in serious storytelling studies; festivals, workshops, and university courses have made the art form more accessible to teachers. Certainly, storytelling fits perfectly in a whole language curriculum. Thus, it may seem unnecessary to set forth a rationale for oral telling in schools; however, certain points need to be acknowledged if we are to appreciate fully the aesthetic effect of storytelling.

To make sense of the world around them, people read, reflect, listen, talk with the family, chatter with friends, play games, and construct fantasy worlds. These activities all involve telling stories to themselves and others. Storytelling is a powerful way to satisfy the human tendency to organize experience. This ancient art of interpreting life through incident and metaphor not only entertains but instructs and imparts wisdom.

Reading stories has its own advantages: the reader may linger over or reread passages, with time to reflect; illustrations are a potent and appealing force in setting meaning. Conversely, storytelling more directly challenges students' minds to find meaning in the story. The storyteller's voice has the power to evoke meaning. Understanding and response are of the moment. Images form in the mind's eye, more actively engaging the listener in picturing the story's events. The story that is told is only available for reflection in memory, after the event, so story listening becomes a complete, rounded, and contained experience from beginning to end.

More important, storytelling is a community experience. Whether the audience is large or a single person, the act of sharing a story is empowering to teller and receiver. Each listener responds personally, with particular mental images and associations. The teller is confirmed as one who imparts wisdom and as the one who has the power to establish that captivating link of intimacy that hovers in the air between storyteller and audience. Beyond these effects, when students talk freely among themselves in the classroom about stories heard, each response enhances the others—a truly interactive experience. From this sharing, student's original stories, written or dictated, will be richer in description, action, and setting.

Exploring how students make meaning from stories is one of the most important aspects of storytelling in the classroom. Consider the variety of images in the following responses from nine- and ten-year-old students who participated in a storytelling study.[1] The story is of a poor man who sought the help of a witch—described by the storyteller only as "a wise old woman who had both black and white magic." Students responded to the researcher's question, "Tell me the pictures you saw in your head as I told the story":

> She was a big, black witch, in a big, black costume with a big, black pot and a crystal on the shelf.

> I didn't think she looked like a witch. She was sitting at a desk with one of those chairs that goes way back.

> She was in a dungeon, and I could see bones in her pot, and the bones spelled out "boy," "girl."

She was a short, fat lady with a whole bunch of wrinkles.

She had a long nose, a big wart, long hair, ugly orange hat, a green shirt, blue and black pants on—a messy Tessie.

It is evident that the responses above were formed not only from literary experience (e.g., black pot, big wart) but also from experiential background (e.g., one of those chairs that goes way back, messy Tessie). It is not surprising that each "witch" is an intensely personal image. The question is, how will that image affect that student's expectations and perceptions of the woman's actions in the story?

This question suggests that meaning resides in far more than memory of story structure. Story maps and structure charts are valid ways of exploring how stories work, but story comprehension should not stop there. When students are encouraged to freely share their immediate responses to stories heard, the teacher's insight will be far more accurate and useful than results from right or wrong answers to structured questions. When teachers engage students in a wide variety of story experiences and give them opportunities to respond in varied ways, teacher and students, together, will embark on an exciting and rewarding journey.

Finding Stories Good for Telling

It does matter what stories we tell. The purpose for telling, the audience, and the occasion are all crucial considerations. Perhaps most important is recognizing that stories with the power to engage both teller and listeners will be more memorable and meaningful.

How is a story found that has this quality and that will "tell" well? In the end, it must be a happy marriage between teller and tale:

1. The first criterion is *never* to try telling a story you do not like, even if it fits a curricular unit perfectly; the story must speak to you in some way. Perhaps the characters are appealing; the setting may strike a responsive note; the theme may be worthwhile; or the story may simply be wonderfully funny. Usually it is a combination of elements. Whatever the appeal, you should have a strong sense that this is a story you want to tell.

2. The story should also have qualities of excitement, laughter, poignancy, or other appeals to the listener. When a story touches the human condition in a meaningful way, the listener's response will be meaningful.

3. Look for a well-paced plot and interesting dialogue that sounds right to you. Stories for telling have more action than description. Literary tales with leisurely descriptions are better saved for reading, but such descriptive passages can be condensed into a few sentences for storytelling.

4. When selecting a folktale, be sure it is faithful to the culture. Consider all aspects of the story: events, characters, setting, language, theme, and imagery. Check the editor's credentials on the book jacket or in a reference source. If a collection of folktales includes notes, usually following the stories, there is good indication that the editor respects the culture's traditions.

5. When choosing a story, either traditional or contemporary, in picture-book format, consider the illustrations. Will they inform your telling, or does your vision of the story differ substantially from that of the artist?

These are broad suggestions for choosing stories aside from their musical possibilities. Appendix A lists titles readily available in libraries or bookstores that, in our experience, fall within these criteria. Appendix B is a bibliography of stories that are appropriate for musical scoring or that already include music of some sort.

MUSIC IN THE CLASSROOM

"Music is the house that sounds live in." A young girl created this striking metaphor, which tells us that music is sound, living in some kind of structure. It is open-ended, allowing for organization from simple clapping exercises to complex symphonic masterpieces.

The Processes of Music

For any musical experience to be worthwhile, the music must mean something to the individual. This can transpire in many different ways, so a variety of musical activities are suggested in hopes that musical needs can be filled for a wide range of ages and abilities.

In this "house of music" are three elements: the composer—the organizer of sounds (the architect), the performer—the transmitter of sounds (the builder), and the listener—the receiver of sounds (the inhabitant). Students who participate in all three areas will have successful experiences in music making. Thus, any good music program should enable students to explore all facets of music and find individual strengths therein.

The intangible state of music is both an asset and a liability. It is an asset for giving us freedom to imagine stories, pictures, and other connections. It is a liability because we cannot see or touch music. In the merging of spoken word and musical sound, both art forms are enhanced and heightened, allowing participants to gain greater meaning and joy from the arts.

The Composer

The composer organizes sounds to create a piece of music. Compositional exercises allow the student to become actively involved in the music-making process. Although the professional composer is a highly trained and gifted individual, anyone can "compose" at their own level. All students can organize sounds, and there are a multitude of ways to organize sounds to create a piece of music, such as emphasizing an element or sound, repeating a phrase, or timing the sounds. This book provides many suggestions for organizing sounds. The compositional process will naturally incorporate the other two elements in the "house of music": listening, to critique and respond to the music, and performing, to make the composition come to life.

Improvisation is when the sounds are loosely organized and not notated specifically. Usually, improvisation is spontaneous, with just a few guidelines. There is a great amount of freedom in an improvisational activity. It can serve as a one-time exercise or as the base for a more involved composition. The composer also is the performer in improvisation.

Composition involves more thought. Ideas are notated so that a performer can play the musical piece. Therefore, not as much freedom is found in a musical composition.

Both improvisations and compositions can be created to explore a musical idea, tell a story, express or evoke a mood, or reflect on an event, for example.

The Performer

The performer's task is to relay the composer's intent to the listener. Sometimes the performer is the composer, but many times not. The performer's role is highly specialized, and few people make their livelihood through performing. However, all students can perform using sounds they make or create.

For many, performing is satisfying and enjoyable, for it engages one in the most active music-making experience. With several activities in this book, performing is paired with composing or listening experiences.

The Listener

As any performer can tell you, if there is no one to listen, there is no reason to make the music, for music is a means of expression and is how a performer communicates. "Attending to" is a phrase that describes a listener's role in the musical experience. It is not a passive role but an active mental process that will occur during a listening experience if the stage has been carefully prepared.

The listening experiences in this book are intended to give students active mental experiences so that listening becomes meaningful to them. A variety of suggested recordings for listening appear throughout this book.

Choosing Music

The kind of music you choose for listening experiences depends on what your objectives are. For each listening activity (most are in chapter 1, but they can be found throughout the book), there is a concept supporting that activity. However, these activities can be adapted for a specific curricular goal. Perhaps you are presenting a unit on water. Many exercises in the book can be adapted for this theme. A general classroom teacher may decide to collaborate with a music specialist to guide students through more extensive listening experiences such as those found in chapter 3.

For each listening activity, musical examples are given. Many of these recordings are available at public libraries. There are usually several different versions of each selection, with some specific recordings listed. Also, collections and anthologies of recordings such as *The Greatest Hits of the Baroque Period*, *Mozart's Greatest Hits*, or *Weekend Classics* encompass a wide variety of selections supporting the title.

If the activity involves an element of music like a rhythm pattern or melody, you can choose music of any style or origin. There is an abundance of traditional Western music listed in the activities. Only in the last few years have music specialists begun to accept non-Western music for more than its exotic appeal.

The range and scope of music from other cultures warrants an exploration that is beyond the scope of this book, but we encourage teachers to explore the music of other cultures on their own, creating new or derivative activities for their students. A brief section on traditional music of other cultures ("Musical World Map") is included in chapter 4, and lists of sample recordings for classroom use are included in reference sections at the end of chapters 1-4 as well as in appendix C. "General Guidelines for Listening" can be found in chapter 1. A social studies and geography curriculum should include music and instruments from countries and areas studied to heighten understanding of the people who live in those areas.

Finding Sounds

Many activities in this book deal with finding sounds, an important facet of music. *Found sounds* are any sounds that are around and available at any given moment. Each environment has its own found sounds. You have them in your purse, classroom, backyard, and kitchen. Found sounds are not musical instruments, like a piano or a voice. They usually have another primary function. Right now, open your purse, desk, or drawer and find as many sounds as you can. Perhaps you find keys, a pen, coins, a ruler, or some hard candy. All of these make interesting found sounds. Found sounds are usually percussive (although an egg slicer makes a terrific mini-harp!).

People have two primary ways to make sounds—*body percussion* and *vocal sounds*. Body percussion includes clapping, snapping, hitting feet, patting knees, and so on. Vocal sounds include whistling, buzzing lips, humming, singing (nonsense syllables, vowels, consonants), growling, and smacking lips.

Along with body percussion and vocal sounds, found sounds are the easiest, handiest, and most inexpensive sounds to use for musical activities. They also challenge students and promote creative-thinking skills. Chapter 2 has a number of activities utilizing body, vocal, and found sounds.

A notch above found sounds are musical instruments created from found sounds and found objects. These may require a little manipulation and are not as easily accessible. Some examples would be hitting a pan with a spoon, hitting two spoons together, rattling dry beans in a yogurt container, and scraping corrugated cardboard with a plastic margarine-container top that has been cut in half. There are many good books with simple instructions on making homemade instruments. Chapter 5 has many examples of instruments to make.

Next in complexity are classroom instruments. These are not toys but simple, sturdy, musical instruments that can enhance a sound composition. Many music stores carry classroom instruments. Appendix D lists suggested stores and suppliers. These instruments can be inexpensive (plastic recorders cost about $2.00) or costly (a solid-wood bass xylophone can cost several hundred dollars). A good starting set of classroom instruments (if money were no object) would include the following:

assorted hand drums

tambourine

guiro (scraping instrument)

soprano glockenspiel

soprano xylophone

alto xylophone

bass xylophone

slide whistle

wood blocks

soprano recorder (third grade and up)

pair of bongos

wind chimes

finger cymbals

triangle

Most of these instruments are easy to use and are great for many sound compositions and story orchestrations.

Finally, we come to actual musical instruments such as the piano, flute, violin, and guitar. The piano has great possibilities without needing instruction, but most other orchestral instruments require formal training. An autoharp is effective for sound compositions and stories. An instrument that has become more affordable in recent years is a keyboard synthesizer. It is great for effects in music and story combinations. You do not need one with a lot of keys but rather one with a range of sound possibilities. If students play musical instruments, find ways to incorporate their talents into the activities.

Skills Needed

Music can be created, performed, and enjoyed on many levels. For the teacher, a basic understanding of the musical elements—rhythm, melody, harmony, timbre, structure (repetition and contrast), and expressiveness (dynamics, tempo) are required. Chapter 2 gives definitions and activities to help teachers and students understand these concepts. Note-reading or instrument-playing is not a requirement. Neither is it necessary to possess a "good singing voice" to use voice effectively. Do not let insecurities about "carrying a tune" get in the way of using this handy instrument for musical activities. Too many of us had music teachers in the past who made us feel inadequate about our music-making abilities. Please do not let that hinder your work with students.

Students do not need to know how to read music for the activities in this book. Devising notation as a means of remembering a musical thought can be done with symbols, lines, letters, or any other way your students wish. Chapter 3 provides several exercises in creating ways to write music.

A critical skill for activities that involve steady rhythmic patterns is a sense of musical pulse. Young children who have been given opportunities to respond to steady rhythmic patterns can keep with an external pulse and feel musical phrases and patterns much more easily than those who have not had such opportunities. If students cannot keep a steady beat when working with steady rhythms, there are ways to help them. Using the right kind of music (e.g., any of the High/Scope folk music recordings, the *Hooked on Classics* series that juxtaposes a steady rock beat with classical recordings, or vintage rock and roll recordings such as the Beatles, etc.; see appendix C for an extensive list of suggestions) with rhythm stick games, hand jive patterns, follow the leader, and movement games can be fun, educational activities. Chapter 1 has some activities for working on keeping the beat. Phyllis Weikert's books are also helpful (see "Music Education and Theory" in appendix B).

NOTES

1. Barbara M. Britsch, "Walking Around Inside Stories: How Children Make Meaning from Narrative Discourse" (unpublished Ph.D. diss., University of Toledo, Ohio, 1990).

PART
I

Responding

It may be said that there are two ways to reflect on or respond to a work of art: looking at the forest or looking at the trees. Most of the experiences in this chapter involve looking at the forest, that is, the gestalt or the whole effect of the work upon the responder. It is primarily a right-brain experience. Looking at the trees, or pulling-apart, logical, and technical analysis, is discussed in chapter 2. We believe that a holistic response to a work of art is an appropriate way to begin.

In this chapter's activities, we will explore the effect of a work of art on us as individuals. This is what aesthetics is all about—a work of art's meaning to the perceiver. "Attending to" a work of art is challenging but absolutely necessary if one is to make sense of the work and find value in it.

Our intent in this chapter is to offer ways for students to develop and feel a sense of ownership of a work of art. This ownership concept will help students become aesthetically literate. Many of these explorations can be adapted for various age groups, as specified with the activity. Following the activities for stories and music separately, you will find several exercises that combine music and stories into a unified response experience.

RESPONDING TO STORIES

Responding to stories heard is both a private and a shared experience. Each student's constructed images, predictions, and personal responses shape that listener's story experience. Then, the sharing of these images and responses in informal talk about the story leads students to respect individual visions and to realize that the story has many possibilities for meaning.

The importance of engaging students in lively, informal discussion immediately following the reading or telling of a story cannot be overemphasized. This is the time to allow them free expression, in their own language, of responses that will clarify and expand personal visions. Such conversation will also sanction a range of ideas, as classmates confirm or surprise with a variety of interpretations.

Several of the activities ask students to consider various artists' versions of the same folktale. In this way, students learn that different artists respond to and interpret the same story differently. Contrast, for example, Susan Jeffers's cool palette for *Snow-White and the Seven Dwarfs* and Trina Schart Hyman's darker version of the same story. The force of illustrations is often crucial in the construction of mental images and thus in eliciting a particular response to a story.

The use of language, like the choice and arrangement of notes in a musical piece, is also a force in creating meaning.

> *Nibble, nibble, I hear a mouse.*
> *Who's that nibbling at my house?*

From *The Complete Fairy Tales of the Brothers Grimm* (Zipes), this charming rhyme that Hansel and Gretel hear as they begin to eat from the witch's house gives no hint of coming disaster. A discussion with students of possible alternative greetings may illuminate the force of this one.

By providing students with a variety of response modes to the whole story, teacher and class may explore more fully its possible meanings as well as its aesthetic dimensions.

STORY ACTIVITIES

The following activities are designed to engage students in holistic responses to stories told or read.

Do You See What I See?

Concepts: Developing and enhancing mental imagery during a story.
Acknowledging a variety of responses to a story.

Materials: A story to be told or read.

Ages: 5 and up.

The simplest way to encourage student responses to stories is to ask them to share images created in the mind's eye while listening.

1. If reading a story, do not share the illustrations. Following the story, ask, "Tell me the pictures you saw in your head as I told (read) the story." This question seems to work well with all ages. Further exploration and questioning can be adjusted to student's developmental levels. There are no right or wrong answers. Accept all interpretations seriously. For responses that seem at complete odds with the text, or designed purely to call attention to the speaker, explore the range of possibilities through open-ended questioning, always referring to the story's content and language. Although stories may evoke many responses, they are limited by the dimensions of the text.

2. For more specific exploration, ask about particular characters, settings, or events. Keep questions open-ended. What does (character) look like? What did the cottage (great hall, castle) look like to you? What sounds might the boy have heard in the woods? Hearing a variety of responses will help students to understand that stories have personal meanings, often based on a student's life experiences, and that varying images may all be valid.

3. Keeping simple notes or audiotaping as students talk will give the teacher material for creative writing or other class projects to continue the story adventure. This also will provide an ongoing record of how individual students are responding to stories.

Many Artists, Many Visions

Concepts: Conveying the validity of individual versions of a story. Exploring a story's aesthetic dimensions.

Materials: Two or more picture-book versions of one story.

Ages: 5 and up.

Exploring several artists' versions of the same story gives students a close look at the art of a picture-story book and confirms alternate images of the same tale. Various versions of stories appear in the references at the end of this chapter.

1. Following students' discussion of their mental story images, show them several picture-book versions of one folktale. Tell or read the story if it is unfamiliar. For well-known stories or those previously shared, you may begin with the illustrations, perhaps focusing on the main character or characters first.

2. Compare shapes and sizes, clothing, hair, facial expressions, all aspects that set one version apart from another. For example, Bernadette Watts's semirealistic, highly detailed, soft illustrations for *The Elves and the Shoemaker* contrast startlingly with Paul Galdone's lively cartoon art for the same story. Watts's elves, though smiling, seem very workmanlike, and Galdone's, conceived in broader strokes, appear more antic. The purpose is not to conclude that one is better than another, merely different, each with its own appropriateness.

3. The use of color is important in distinguishing these interpretations. The cool, rich colors of Nancy Ekholm Burkert in Randall Jarrell's *Snow-White and the Seven Dwarfs* contrast directly with the shadowy, darker colors of Trina Schart Hyman in Paul Heins's version. The first keeps us at a distance; the second draws us in, partly with color and partly with other aesthetic elements such as style, number of illustrations, and how the queen's face portrays her increasing anxiety.

4. For younger students, explore simple differences of obvious physical characteristics, focusing on the concrete. Various editions of Mother Goose rhymes work well for this. Older students can analyze more subtle elements such as the use of shadow, placement of text on the page in relation to the art, and various art styles such as cartoon, realistic, or impressionistic. For these students, relate the illustrations to the text, discussing how each artist portrays the same event, characters, and so on, differently and how each version affects our response to the story.

5. Older students can explore how folktales are portrayed by undertaking a serious study of folklore, perhaps from a particular culture, or by studying the aesthetics of picture books as an art form.

6. Place the books in the classroom library or at a learning center and encourage students to compare them at leisure. Art projects hooked to the story are a natural continuation. Younger students may design their own characters and/or setting, experimenting with cutouts, crayons, or markers for various effects. Older students may complete a full-page illustration for the story in a style complementary to or different from those studied or design book pages incorporating text and art. (Instructions for bookbindings are found in chapter 6.) You may also ask students to design a new cover. Compare and discuss the varying effects each cover might have on a reader, not judgmentally, but focusing on strengths.

The crucial aspect of the preceding activities is to encourage freehand efforts, rather than giving the class commercial cutouts to decorate or stencils to trace. Younger students, particularly, should be discouraged from trying to copy book illustrations in the mistaken belief that these are better than their own efforts.

Did You Lose It?

Concepts: Exploring characters and plot through movement that transforms the abstract into the concrete.

Materials: *The Funny Little Woman* (Mosel).

Ages: 7 and up.

This activity asks students to investigate characterization and story events through creative movement and improvisational drama. As actors understand: "What my body learns through movement, my mind will understand."

1. Tell or read *The Funny Little Woman*. In this Japanese folktale, a woman hunting for a lost dumpling is led into a great adventure. Discuss the frustration of losing something, eliciting examples from students. You may wish to list these on the chalkboard.

2. Ask students to imagine they are hunting a lost object or animal. Is it dangerous? (a wolf) Is it small? (a crayon) Does it have a sound? (an alarm clock) Then ask them to imagine where they are hunting: in the woods, a park, their room, the classroom, or a cave? Ask them to imagine how they are hunting: opening drawers, looking under buses, tracking quietly, moving furniture, or on tiptoe?

3. Once they have decided what they are hunting, where they are looking, and how, ask each student to move across the front of the classroom, one at a time, pantomiming the hunt as the class watches carefully, noting as many details as possible. The emphasis is not on guessing but on being able to "see" shapes, sizes, locations, and so on. To slow down students' tendency to rush through a mime, suggest they do it in slow motion.

4. Ask students to suggest body shapes and movements for the woman, the statues, and the Oni in the story. Show these in a freeze with small groups and discuss the various possibilities. Improvise one scene from the story in mime as a narrator reads it, perhaps the woman's walk down the street of statues or her escape from the Oni. It is possible to have several "little women" and many Oni to allow more participation. Each scene, however, must have an audience.

5. Develop the whole story in mime with narration. Encourage students to find unique characterizations and maintain them consistently. Focus on one physical characteristic at first, perhaps a certain walk (limping, strutting), to help students get started with this idea. A hand motion or facial movement such as winking or raising an eyebrow may then be added. Start simply, then add. Encourage the class to avoid imitating current movie or TV favorites in designing postures and movements. Remind them that this is "once upon a time" in a far away country. Blair Lent's illustrations for this book may be consulted for ideas, if desired.

6. A variation is to use several of the students' original pantomimes (hunting a lost object) to develop a class story, following the sequence of events in *The Funny Little Woman*: loss, hunt, capture, escape, return home. Improvise it in mime with narration, again being careful to be consistent in characterization.

There's a Monster in My Classroom

Concepts: Demonstrating an understanding of a character and his or her actions by transposing them from a known story to an original story.

Materials: *Where the Wild Things Are* (Sendak), felt board and felt monster pieces (hands, feet, legs, torso, etc.), drawing materials (crayons, markers, paper, etc.), small pieces of paper, straight pins.

Ages: 5-7.

Beginning with a visual component, this activity encourages story composition and story illustration.

1. Tell or read *Where the Wild Things Are*. With the book at hand, discuss with students the appearance of Sendak's "wild things": their teeth, ears, tails, claws, general shapes, and so on.

2. Ask students to create two or three monsters on a felt board, with each student placing a felt piece where they wish. If an arm ends up where an ear might logically be, fine! We are not trying to duplicate Sendak's monsters or normal body configurations.

3. Again with the book, look at the mischief Max does (e.g., nails in the wall, harassing the dog) and imagine what kinds of mischief the created monsters might do. Keep a list of the students' decisions.

4. Ask students to suggest names for each created monster, printing the name on a small piece of paper and pinning it to the felt board. They might also wish to add the place where each creature lives and its favorite food. Keep this "monster board" on display.

5. Another day, construct a simple class story orally for one or more of these creatures, beginning with the information on the board and the "mischief list." Guide the story carefully so that it has a few easily identifiable episodes and is not too long. From your notes, retell the story with the class, briefly identifying the beginning, each event, and the ending. List the events on the chalkboard and review.

6. Ask students to draw the story's events, one per student. Duplicate drawings are fine; they offer you the chance to point out how the same event is imagined differently. Connect the pages in order and hang the story as a banner or frieze in the classroom. The story is now available for retelling, even dramatizing. Repeat, if necessary, until all monsters are in a story. The felt board is then freed for other uses.

The Color of Stories

Concepts: Encouraging creative, right-brain questioning. Conceptualizing a story in terms of other media, objects, or events.

Materials: A variety of folktales suitable in length and complexity for the intended audience (see references at the end of this chapter).

Ages: 10 and up.

This is not so much a single activity as an ongoing approach to telling folktales. You may combine these questions with others, such as those asking for mental imagery (see the activity "Do You See What I See?" in this chapter). By keeping a record, written or taped, of students' responses, you will gradually acquire a list of words and phrases that can be shared with students in a discussion of the effect of various stories on the listener.

Now is the time to sharpen the ability to tell, not read, a story. Voice, gestures, and facial expressions have everything to do with making the story come alive and with eliciting honest responses.

1. Choose folktales with varying tones and emotional landscapes: a spooky story; a sharp, bright trickster tale; a myth or creation story; a fable; a story with distinctive character voices.

2. After each story, ask the following questions to encourage student participation in discussion and comparisons. It is important that students defend their answers.

   If this story were a color, what would it be? Why?

   If this story were a piece of music, what would it sound like?

   If this story were weather, what would the sky look like?

   If this story were a kind of food, what would it taste like?

The following set of questions may prove more challenging:

_____ fit like _____ .
(story title)   (a piece of clothing)

_____ sounded like _____ .
(story title)   (a holiday)

_____ moved like _____ .
(story title)   (mode of transportation)

3. After presenting different types of stories, initiate a discussion of students' responses. Use both their language and the story text to explore how responses are shaped by story contents (actions, events) as well as language, descriptions, and settings. Compare language and dialogue from the story with students' responses.

4. Older students may complete the following paragraph in writing after hearing a story for the first time. This is a very supportive activity, for students may imagine what they wish (there are no wrong answers). Have students provide a short paragraph from the following ideas.

> In the beginning of the story, I wanted to know_____.
>
> I would like to ask the main character _____.
>
> If I could walk through this story, the ground would feel like _____.
>
> I would like to compose _____music for this story.
>
> If I could prepare food for the characters, I would cook _____.
>
> At the end, I felt _____.

RESPONDING TO MUSIC

Teachers can help students learn the art of active listening to music in several ways. The importance of "attending to" a piece of music has been discussed in the introduction. The following activities promote active listening experiences in a manner that increases creative thinking about a piece of music. These activities focus on responses that reflect the wholeness of the work rather than technique or analysis. Active listening and responding experiences for the latter can be found in chapter 3.

As with stories, images are a valuable tool for enabling students to respond to music. These images usually arise from personal experiences of the listener. Therefore, at different levels, the responses will reflect those experiences.

The following are three forms of responding to music:

1. *Visual*: Images, both abstract and concrete, that reflect the mood or overall feeling of the piece, illustrate a technical aspect (form, repetition, melody) or tell a story (real or imagined).

2. *Verbal:* Specific answers to questions about the music, metaphors, or symbolic language that refer to something occurring or a story created in response to the music.

3. *Kinesthetic:* Rhythmic and creative movement to the music (both overall and specific elements).

Because young students' verbal abilities are not fully developed, visual and kinesthetic responses work especially well with this age group. However, not having a musical vocabulary should not be a deterrent to verbal responses for any age. The use of metaphor, simile, creative questioning, and so on can overcome this language barrier. It is of little value for the student to understand that "accelerando" means to speed up if he cannot recognize that occurring in a piece of music. Far better for the student to describe the music as sounding like "a car getting up to speed on an entrance ramp to a freeway," which tells us it accelerated.

Keep in mind when eliciting responses from students that they have every right to dislike the music. However, their response must justify why they dislike it. "I think it's boring and dumb" is not an acceptable response. "I prefer music that uses more brass instruments and has a faster tempo" is acceptable because it shows that the student understands what the piece is about musically.

Music: An Art Form Taken for Granted?

Our sense of hearing can be greatly underused in modern society because excess sound pollution encourages us at times to shut our ears. Part of the sound pollution is the "wallpaper" music that we are constantly exposed to in movies and on TV, during sporting events, on elevators, on telephones, and in doctors' offices, to name a few. This use of music dilutes its importance as an art form. We begin to take music for granted and think of it as an adjunct or embellishment to a more important event. Teachers can give students opportunities to experience good music and guide them in making sense of this most accessible yet most abstract of all art forms.

Directed Listening

Because listening is perceived as a passive approach to music (rather than "hands-on"), listening would seem to be the most difficult music activity for achieving participation with students. However, most people's involvement with music is an *appreciation*—through listening (live performances or electronic productions). Music is important because of its fundamental purpose—music is a "basic means for making full contact with reality."[1] But *studying* music grants the listener significant functional connections: to the peoples of the world, to the learning process, to the imagination, and to art. Music is a basic means of communication and self-expression.[2]

These aesthetic and functional reasons for the pursuit of music emphasize the importance of establishing good listening skills in students at an early age. Obviously, appropriate listening skills should be developed in music classes, but if a music specialist is not on the staff, classroom teachers can use the following guidelines when conducting a listening activity with any piece of music.

General Guidelines for Listening

1. Keep talking to a minimum while music is playing. Give all pertinent information before you begin the music. Show by example that when music is playing, whether recorded or live, the focus is on listening.

2. Choose music that is short enough to keep students' attention but long enough to be of value. You might wish to play just one movement of a longer piece.

3. Play the same piece of music several times. The first time, play it as students enter the room, just for exposure. The next time, play it with a specific listening task. The third time, play it after discussing the task at hand and confirming the musical aspects in question to reinforce students' understanding of the music. After this kind of comprehensive listening approach, students should be ready to make a critical judgment of the piece and suggest its meaning.

MUSIC ACTIVITIES

Every Picture Tells a (Musical) Story

Concepts: Using pictures as a bridge for understanding a musical work.

Materials: Various pictures from magazines; museum postcards; musical selection: *Trois Pièces Brèves for Wind Quartet* (Ibert), *Two Part Inventions* (Bach), *Für Elise* (Beethoven), or *Pierrot Lunaire* (Schoenberg).

Ages: 5 and up.

This activity is a good way to explore a piece of music with students, who may not know musical terminology. It is up to the teacher to interpret their visual responses to the musical idea being represented. The suggested recordings are just that—suggestions. Feel free to use any music you wish that expresses one overall mood.

1. For an initial, general interpretation, play the music and, as it is playing, show several pictures of contrasting nature (e.g., a pastoral scene versus a storm at sea, a jungle of vegetation versus a barren desert). Reproductions of paintings in magazines such as *Yankee*, and the vivid photographs in *National Geographic*, are excellent for this activity. They are subjective, easy to comprehend, and large enough for the entire class to see when mounted on poster boards. After the music is finished, elicit responses as to which picture best fit the music and why, leading into exploration of musical effect, musical elements, controls-dynamics, tempo, volume, orchestration, melody, and rhythm. This may be a superficial analysis, but it allows the class an entrance into the piece.

The following variations can be adapted in many ways for more advanced students.

2. Variation: When an obvious change in the music occurs (tempo, instrumentation, dynamics, etc.), you can select a different picture to represent that change.

3. Variation: If sections of the music repeat, use the same picture, which will help students visualize the form. (See chapter 3 for more activities on form analysis.)

4. Variation: Abstract artwork can also be used, with colors, lines, shapes, and patterns representing musical effect as well as specific elements.

An Artist's Inspiration

Concepts: Evaluating students' understanding of a musical work.

Materials: Abstract, colorful shapes cut out of paper and laminated, one for each student; musical recordings: "Andante" from *Suite no. 1 for Small Orchestra* and *Fanfare for a New Theatre for Two Trumpets* (Stravinsky).

Ages: 8 and up.

This exercise involves creating a visual response while listening to music. The two selections by Stravinsky work well for contrasting moods, but you may choose any two pieces. There are many suggestions in appendix C.

1. Give each student a colorful shape of paper. (We use shapes inspired by the French artist Henri Matisse, who used free-form cutouts in many of his works.)

2. In a large, empty space, have students stand in a circle. The middle is the blank canvas. While the music is playing, students quietly place their shapes down when they wish or upon a nonverbal signal from the teacher. When the music is completed, everyone looks at the "painting" from all angles. Discuss not only the finished artwork and its relationship to the music but also the process of creating the artwork. Why did they place their shapes where they did, when they did, and in that manner? Again, this would reveal students' feeling and understanding of the overall message of the music, not necessarily the formal structure of the composition.

3. Follow the same procedure for the second piece of music and compare the two artworks.

4. With younger students, adapt this idea by using a large felt board with many colorful shapes. One at a time, students can place their felt piece on the board as their response to the music.

Which Is Which?

Concepts: Evaluating students' recognition of musical styles.

Materials: Three different art materials (colored markers, pastel crayons, stickers, watercolors, fluorescent markers, etc.), a sheet of paper with nine squares drawn on it (one for each student), recorded music (see below).

Ages: 5-8.

This is an excellent activity to get students involved in the listening process. Find three distinctly contrasting pieces of music with obvious differences. Examples are a fanfare by Lully or Gabrieli (bright, loud, exciting, dramatic; Gabrieli is featured on *Music from the Renaissance and Baroque*, played by the Royal Brass, and on *Baroque Favorites*); "Clair de Lune" by Debussy (calm, peaceful, soft, light); and *Poème Electronique* by Varèse (contemporary, discordant). Tape three samples from each selection, approximately thirty to forty-five seconds each time. Record about ten seconds of silence between each sample so that there are nine musical examples in random sequence.

1. With the three types of art materials, discuss what each material would represent if it were sound. For instance, pastel crayons might remind students of light, airy, quiet sounds; colored markers might suggest bright, loud, clashy sounds; and glittery, shiny stickers might remind them of weird, unusual, "outer space" sounds.

2. Explain that each material will represent a type of music and discuss the feeling of each of the types. Briefly describe the kinds of music they will hear and which art material will be used when they hear each type of music. Explain the sequence of squares or have students number the squares from one to nine. Students will start in square one with the first selection, square two for the second, until their paper is full. They should only use the selected art materials when they hear the represented musical sound. During the silence, students should move to the next square. Remind students to listen *before* determining which art material they will use. Keep all talking to a minimum so students rely on their ears. This really works and is great fun!

Moving Through Space

Concepts: Using movement for evaluating musical understanding.

Materials: Strands of tiny Christmas lights; musical selection: any from *Glassworks* (Glass), *Down to the Moon* (Vollenweider), or "Air on a G String" (Bach).

Ages: 5 and up.

This is a creative movement activity allowing students a gestalt-like experience to music. Movement is a vehicle by which students can express their reaction to and understanding of the music in a nonverbal way.

1. String several strands of small Christmas lights around the room—walls, ceilings, floors, everywhere. Turn off the room lights and turn on the small lights. Play mood music (such as one of the selections above). The darkness and twinkling lights free students to respond spontaneously and explore the space around them. Call out a few directions for movement, or use this as a finishing, relaxation exercise. This activity also can be done using live music, with the musician following the ideas generated by students' movements.

2. When the music ends, discuss with students how the combination of darkness, lights, and music made them feel. Did it free them? Did they feel they were something other than themselves? What other kinds of music would work with this activity? What would not?

Changing Times

Concepts: Discovering universal responses to music.

Materials: Tape of several musical pieces of varying styles (see below).

Ages: All ages.

Tape several short samples of all kinds of music varying in style, tempo, orchestration, and character. Use any recordings you wish or ones from appendix C. The listed collections such as RCA Victor *Greatest Hits* or Victrola *Best Of* series are excellent sources for a variety of styles and moods. The tape should have a slight pause of about five seconds between selections. Use each musical selection only once.

1. If possible, move chairs and desks from the center of the room so there is plenty of space to move.

2. Students can move any way they wish, according to the music being played.

3. One variation is to give each student a streamer to wave while the music is being played.

4. Another variation is for the class to use rhythm sticks and create patterns according to the overall beat of the music.

5. In another variation, for each new selection, the teacher calls out a manner in which to move: backward, bent knees, in a square, on tiptoe, like a cat, and so on.

6. To increase the excitement and make the exercise more like a game for older students, stop the tape between pieces and call out an instruction in which students are to group: according to birth month, color of socks, favorite food, least favorite subject, and so on. Give them only ten seconds to find their group before you start the tape again.

Freeze Frame

Concepts: Sharpening basic listening skills.

Materials: Taped music with random pauses of silence inserted.

Ages: 5-6.

Use this tape in a variety of ways to increase students' basic response to hearing sounds and silence. Instrumental music works best. Choose any piece of music you wish. Push the pause button on the tape recorder to make the pauses.

1. Students move freely around room and freeze whenever there is silence.

2. During the silence, give directions for a movement when the music begins again.

3. A variation is to use beanbags or rhythm sticks. Toss or hit to the rhythm and freeze during silence.

4. Another variation is to sit in a circle and use body percussion to the beat of the music. After the silence, change the type of body percussion. Students follow teacher's lead.

What's in a Word?

Concepts: Describing a piece of music.

Materials: Printed statement, chalkboard, any musical selection that you wish to explore.

Ages: Questions and statements—5 and up. Paragraphs—9 and up.

Using questions, statements, and paragraphs is another way students can express their thoughts about music without needing a sophisticated vocabulary or understanding of music. These exercises are best when used as a first-time listening experience so that answers are spontaneous rather than "right." From these answers, help students begin to draw musical conclusions and interpret the work analytically.

1. Before the music begins, ask one of the following questions. After the music is finished, have students present and defend their responses.

   What flower does this music remind you of? _____ .

   If this music were a color, it would be _____ .

   If this music were in a cartoon, you would see _____.

   This music moves like _____(mode of transportation).

   If this music were a holiday, it would be _____.

   If this music were a pet, it would be a _____.

   This music tastes like _____.

For older students:

The music fits like _____ (article of clothing).

The music reminds me of _____ (historical event).

2. Have older students complete the following sentences after they listen to a piece of music for the first time. This open-ended assignment is nonthreatening, for students are not required to use musical terminology.

The music was _____.

As I listened, I thought about _____.

The music kept _____.

After a while it _____.

People around me were _____.

At the end, I felt _____.

This activity is a springboard for further discovery of the musical work. It allows students to voice or describe their reactions and gives the teacher an opportunity to evaluate their general response to the work and decide what to explore further about the music.

COLLABORATIVE ACTIVITIES

The activities in this chapter so far have introduced stories and music separately to students. With the following exercises, students can begin to explore similar responses to elements in stories and music simultaneously.

Tell Me a Story

Concepts: Responding to a combination of music and story.

Materials: Recordings of stories with musical accompaniment (see below).

Ages: 6 and up.

Many recordings are available of popular fables, tales, and stories that students should be familiar with. Most are on the Windham Hill label and feature noted actors and actresses reading the stories and excellent composers creating the musical scores. There are also stories such as Kenneth Grahame's *The Wind in the Willows* and *The Reluctant Dragon*, both scored by John Rutter, that feature a good deal of singing. We have listed many available recordings at the end of this chapter, but consult Windham Hill Records directly for up-to-date information (see appendix D).

1. Choose a story and have the whole class listen. Do not use as background, or students will not concentrate on the combination of words with music. Perhaps have picture-book versions of the story available for comparison after the listening. You might also want to go through the steps described earlier in the activity "Do You See What I See?" Before starting the tape, ask students to listen not only to the story line but also to how the music goes with the story, as there will be discussion afterward about how the two complement each other.

2. After the story is completed, ask the following questions: "What made the combination of music and stories effective? Was there a certain instrument, sound, or melody associated with any of the characters? Did the music contribute to the development of the story or was it just background?" Discuss choice of sounds: Were they appropriate? These questions will vary, depending on the age level of students, but even very young students will be able to recognize how certain sounds and musical events can enhance the meaning of the story.

3. In chapters 3 and 4 you will find activities that allow students to create their own combinations of stories and music.

They Sound Like . . .

Concepts: Enhancing aural perception.

Materials: Any story shared with the class, rhythm instruments that produce a variety of sounds (drums, rattles, bells, tambourines, etc.).

Ages: 5-8.

This activity incorporates the concept of words being expressed through musical sounds in a story setting.

1. After telling or reading a folktale to the class, demonstrate the sound of each instrument and ask students which sound would best represent each character in the story.

2. Using one instrument at a time, ask the class how that character might walk or move to that sound. Try one at a time, with the entire class moving as a particular character to the sound of the chosen instrument. At this point, you may wish to discuss each character more fully.

3. Following this, advanced students may volunteer to cast a short scene from the story. With the appropriate instruments, each character provides accompaniment for the dialogue. Or students may choose to let the instrument speak for them. This should involve some discussion before or after regarding appropriate tempos and rhythms for each character's "words." Don't worry about movement during the scene. The important point is the connection of a specific sound to a character and their relationship. This important combination is explored more fully in chapters 2, 3, and 4.

If This Story Were a Piece of Music

Concepts: Revealing similar aesthetic properties of music and stories.

Materials: Picture books with few or no words (see below), musical selections (see below).

Ages: 5 and up.

This is not so much an activity as it is a way of perceiving artwork. It is a challenge to think about a piece of music or a story in a nontraditional manner.

1. The arts have that special quality of communicating without explaining. At times it is just enough to listen, enjoy, and become enriched through listening to a classic story or piece of music. What becomes extra special is combining a story and musical work that have similar aesthetic qualities. Below is a short list of wonderful picture books that are wordless or have few words. These picture books are paired with accompanying pieces of music. Both art forms share similar aesthetic qualities: tone, rhythm, timbre, and expression. Play the music as you turn the pages of the book for the class. The combining of the two art forms has a powerful force that enhances the understanding for students of both the story and the sound.

Suggested Picture Book	Suggested Music
Dawn by Uri Shulevitz	"Sunrise" by Grofé (from *Grand Canyon Suite*)
I See a Song by Eric Carle	Eine Kleine Nachtmusik, final movement, by Mozart (from *Compact Mozart*)
Rosie's Walk by Pat Hutchins	Children's March by Grainger
The Snowman by Raymond Briggs	"Snowflakes Are Dancing" by Debussy (from *Children's Corner Suite*)
Tuesday by David Weisner	"Ride of the Valkyries" by Wagner (from *Der Ring des Nibelungen*)

2. Once you are familiar with comprehending dual modalities, it is exciting to come upon a new picture book and think, "For some reason, these illustrations remind me of that piece of music I just heard on the radio. What was that?" Or, "Here I am in a car with the radio on and this piece of music reminds me of that picture book by Eric Carle, but I'm not sure why." Ask students to share such experiences.

Stories from Music

Concepts: Responding to a piece of music. Experiencing the shape of a story and a piece of music.

Materials: Paragraph with blanks to be filled in (see below); musical recording: "Dance of the Toy Flutes" (Tchaikovsky), "Minuet" (Mozart), or "Étude in E Major" (Chopin).

Ages: 9 and up.

Here students engage in a synthesis of story and music and identify the basic shape of a story.

1. Choose a piece of music. Decide how the music best divides into three sections. Each of the following three paragraphs should be answered during the respective sections in the music. Play the music and, as each new section begins, call out the paragraph number to students. Students fill in the blanks while listening. This should be done after an initial hearing and before a thorough analysis of the music. The answers can be musically oriented or not.

In the beginning, I saw _____ floating in the air. It

was _____ . I touched it, and it was _____ .
    (sense of hearing)   (sense of touch)

Later on, the music _____ , and
                  (describe the sounds and what happens)

then _____ .
   (anything)

Finally, near the end, the music _____ , and suddenly it
                       (describe the change)

smelled like _____ .
    (sense of smell)

2. List some or all of students' responses on the chalkboard in seven categories, matching each of the seven blanks. In small groups, have students write a story, using choices from each category and following the established framework of the paragraph above.

3. After sharing stories with the class, discuss with students how even simple tales such as these have a shape: a beginning, a middle where things happen, and an end. The events of this mini-story have a cause-and-effect relationship with each other, making this a creative story rather than a report-like nonfictional recounting of an event, such as a class trip.

NOTES

1. Bennett Reimer, "Justifying Music Education," *Music Educators Journal* (November 1993): 14.

2. Kenneth H. Phillips, "A Stronger Rationale for Music Education," *Music Educators Journal* (September 1993): 17.

REFERENCES

Recordings

Bach, Johann Sebastian. "Air on a G String," from *Bach's Greatest Hits*. RCA 60828-2-RG (CD); 60828-4-RG6 (cassette).

———. *Two Part Inventions BWV 772-786*. Malcolm, harpsichord. Elektra/Nonesuch 71144-4 (cassette).

———. *Two Part Inventions BWV 772-786*. Schiff, piano. London 411974-2 LH (CD).

Ball, Patrick. *The Ugly Duckling*. Windham Hill/Rabbit Ears Storybook Classics WD-0705 (CD); WT-0705 (cassette).

Barber, Samuel. "Adagio for Strings," from *Romantic Favorites for Strings*. New York Philharmonic Orchestra. Bernstein. CBS MYK-38484 (CD); MYT-38484 (cassette).

Baroque Favorites. Dallas Trumpets. Crystal C-232 (cassette).

Beethoven, Ludwig van. *Für Elise, Bagatelle Wo056*. Brendel, piano. Philips 412227-2 PH (CD); 412227-4 PH (cassette).

Best of series. Victrola. Several different recordings featuring a variety of composers.

Chieftains, The. *The Tailor of Gloucester*. Windham Hill/Rabbit Ears Storybook Classics WD-0709 (CD); WT-0709 (cassette).

Chopin, Frédéric. "Étude in E Major," from *Études (24) for Piano, op. 10 and op. 25*. Ashkenazy. London 414127-2LH (CD).

Cooder, Ry. *Pecos Bill*. Windham Hill/Rabbit Ears Storybook Classics WD-0709 (CD); WT-0709 (cassette).

Debussy, Claude. "Snowflakes Are Dancing," from *Children's Corner Suite*. Ulster Orchestra. Tortelier. Chandos CHAN-8756 (CD); ABTD-1395 (cassette).

———. "Clair de Lune," from *Suite Bergamasque*. Philadelphia Orchestra. Ormandy. CBS MGT-30950 (cassette).

Glass, Philip. *Glassworks*. CBS MK-37265 (CD); PMT-37265 (cassette).

Grainger, Percy. *Children's March: Over the Hills and Far Away*. Central Band of the Royal Air Force. EMI Records CDC 7496082 (CD).

Greatest Hits series. RCA Victor. Many different recordings featuring various composers and themes.

Grofé, Ferde. "Sunrise," from *Grand Canyon Suite*. New York Philharmonic Orchestra. Bernstein. CBS MYK-37759 (CD); MYT-37759 (cassette).

Ibert, Jacques. *Trois Pièces Brèves for Wind Quintet*. Tuckwell Quintet. Elektra/Nonesuch 780224 (cassette).

———. *Trois Pièces Brèves for Wind Quintet*. Athena Ensemble. Chandos (Collect) CHAN 6543 (CD).

Isham, Mark. *The Emperor's New Clothes.* Windham Hill/Rabbit Ears Storybook Classics WD-0712 (CD); WT-0717 (cassette).

Kottke, Leo. *Paul Bunyan.* Windham Hill/Rabbit Ears Storybook Classics WD-0717 (CD); WT-0717 (cassette).

Lande, Art. *The Three Little Pigs.* Windham Hill/Rabbit Ears Storybook Classics WD-0713 (CD); WT-0713 (cassette).

Lully, Jean Baptiste. *Marches and Field Music: Music of the Baroque and Classical Periods.* Calig CAL 50844 (CD).

McFerrin, Bobby. *The Elephant's Child.* Windham Hill/Rabbit Ears Storybook Classics WD-0701 (CD); WT-0701 (cassette).

Mozart, Wolfgang Amadeus. *Serenade no. 13 in G, K.525, "Eine Kleine Nachtmusik,"* from *Compact Mozart* (disc 1). Sony Classical 5 SBK45977 (CD).

———. "Serenade no. 13 in G, K.525," from *Eine Kleine Nachtmusik.* Vienna Mozart Ensemble. Boskovsky. London 425874-2 LC (CD); 411846-4 LT (cassette).

———. "Minuet," from *Symphony no. 40 in G, K.550.* London Symphony Orchestra. Abbado. Deutsche Grammophon (Galleria) 415841-2 GGA (CD).

———. "Minuet," from *Symphony no. 40 in G, K.550.* Vienna Philharmonic Orchestra. Bernstein. "Leonard Bernstein Edition" Deutsche Grammophon 431040-2 GBE (CD); 431040-4 GBE (cassette).

Royal Brass. *Music from the Renaissance and Baroque.* Empire Brass. Telarc CD-80257 (CD); CS-30301 (cassette).

Rutter. John. *The Reluctant Dragon.* Masterchord MCK412 (cassette).

———. *The Wind in the Willows.* Masterchord MCK412 (cassette).

Schoenberg, Arnold. *Pierrot Lunaire, op. 21.* Contemporary Chamber Ensemble. Weisberg. Elektra/Nonesuch 71251 (cassette).

———. *Pierrot Lunaire, op. 21.* Nash Ensemble. Rattle. Chandos ABR-1046 (CD).

Story, Tim. *The Legend of Sleepy Hollow.* Windham Hill/Rabbit Ears Storybook Classics. WD-0711 (CD); WT-0711 (cassette).

Stravinsky, Igor. *Fanfare for a New Theatre for Two Trumpets.* London Sinfonietta. Chailly. London 417114-2LH (CD).

———. *Suites nos. 1 and 2 for Small Orchestra.* London Sinfonietta. Chailly. London 417114-2LH (CD).

Taj Mahal. *Brer Rabbit and the Wonderful Tar Baby.* Windham Hill/Rabbit Ears Storybook Classics WD-0716 (CD); WT-0716 (cassette).

Tchaikovsky, Piotr Ilyich. "Dance of the Toy Flutes," from *The Nutcracker Suite, op. 71A.* Suisse Romande. Ansermet. London 417097-4LT (cassette).

———. "Dance of the Toy Flutes," from *The Nutcracker Suite, op. 71A.* New York Philharmonic Orchestra. Bernstein. CBS MYK-37238 (CD); MYT-37238 (cassette).

Varèse, Edgard. *Poème Electronique.* Neuma 450-74 (CD).

Vollenweider, Andreas. *Down to the Moon.* CBS MK-4225 (CD); FMT-4255 (cassette).

Wagner, Richard. "Ride of the Valkyries," from *Der Ring des Nibelungen.* New York Philharmonic Orchestra. Mehta. CBS MDK-44657 (CD); MDT-44657 (cassette).

Winston, George. *The Velveteen Rabbit.* Dancing Cat DCD-3007 (CD); DCT-3007 (cassette).

Books

General

Aardema, Verna. *Who's in Rabbit's House?* Illustrated by Leo Dillon and Diane Dillon. New York: Dial, 1977.

Bang, Molly. *The Paper Crane.* New York: Greenwillow, 1985.

Barton, Bob. *The Storm Wife.* Illustrated by Georgi Yudin. Kingston, Ontario: Quarry Press, 1993.

Briggs, Raymond. *The Snowman.* New York: Random House, 1978.

Brown, Marcia. *Shadow.* New York: Scribner's, 1982.

Carle, Eric. *I See a Song.* New York: Thomas Y. Crowell, 1973.

Hutchins, Pat. *Rosie's Walk.* New York: Macmillan, 1968.

Jarrell, Randall, trans. *The Fisherman and His Wife.* Illustrated by Margot Zemach. New York: Farrar, Straus & Giroux, 1980.

Marshall, James. *Goldilocks and the Three Bears.* New York: Dial, 1988.

McDermott, Gerald. *Arrow to the Sun.* New York: Viking Press, 1974.

Mosel, Arlene. *The Funny Little Woman.* Illustrated by Blair Lent. New York: E. P. Dutton, 1972.

Sendak, Maurice. *Where the Wild Things Are.* New York: Harper & Row, 1963.

Shulevitz, Uri. *Dawn.* New York: Farrar, Straus & Giroux, 1974.

Wahl, Jan. *Tailypo!* Illustrated by Wil Clay. New York: Henry Holt, 1991.

Weisner, David. *Tuesday.* New York: Clarion Books, 1991.

Yolen, Jane. *Tam Lin.* Illustrated by Charles Mikolaycak. San Diego, Calif.: Harcourt Brace Jovanovich, 1990.

Zipes, Jack. *The Complete Fairy Tales of the Brothers Grimm.* Illustrated by John B. Gruelle. New York: Bantam Books, 1987.

Folktales for Comparison

Brett, Jan. *Beauty and the Beast.* New York: Clarion Books, 1989.

Brown, Marcia. *Cinderella.* New York: Scribner's, 1954.

Cauley, Lorinda. *Jack and the Beanstalk.* New York: G. P. Putnam's Sons, 1983.

Climo, Shirley. *The Egyptian Cinderella.* Illustrated by Ruth Heller. New York: HarperCollins, 1989.

dePaola, Tomie. *The Legend of Old Befana.* New York: Harcourt Brace Jovanovich, 1980.

de Regniers, Beatrice Schenk. *Jack and the Beanstalk.* Illustrated by Anne Wilsdorf. New York: Atheneum, 1985.

Edens, Cooper. *Beauty and the Beast.* San Diego, Calif.: Green Tiger Press, 1989.

Galdone, Paul. *The Shoemaker and the Elves.* New York: Clarion, 1984.

Goode, Diane. *Cinderella.* New York: Knopf, 1988.

Haley, Gail. *Jack and the Bean Tree.* New York: Crown, 1986.

Heins, Paul, trans. *Snow White*. Illustrated by Trina Schart Hyman. New York: Little, Brown, 1974.

Hyman, Trina Schart. *Little Red Riding Hood*. New York: Holiday House, 1983.

Jarrell, Randall, trans. *Snow-White and the Seven Dwarfs*. Illustrated by Nancy Ekholm Burkert. New York: Farrar, Straus & Giroux, 1972.

Jeffers, Susan. *Hansel and Gretel*. New York: Dial, 1980.

Karlin, Barbara. *Cinderella*. Illustrated by James Marshall. Boston: Little, Brown, 1989.

Kellogg, Steven. *Jack and the Beanstalk*. New York: Morrow Junior Books, 1991.

Langton, Jane. *The Hedgehog Boy: A Latvian Folktale*. Illustrated by Ilse Plume. New York: Harper & Row.

Lesser, Rika. *Hansel and Gretel*. Illustrated by Paul O. Zelinsky. New York: G. P. Putnam's Sons, 1984.

Lester, Julius. *How Many Spots Does a Leopard Have?* New York: Scholastic, 1989.

Littledale, Freya. *The Elves and the Shoemaker*. Illustrated by Brinton Turkle. New York: Four Winds Press, [c. 1975].

Louie, Ai-Ling. *Yeh-Shen: A Cinderella Story from China*. Illustrated by Ed Young. New York: Philomei Books, 1982.

Martin, Rafe. *The Rough-Face Girl*. Illustrated by David Shannon. New York: G. P. Putnam's Sons, 1992.

Mayer, Marianna. *Beauty and the Beast*. New York: Macmillan, 1987.

Mikolaycak, Charles. *Babushka*. New York: Holiday House, 1984.

Plume, Ilse. *The Shoemaker and the Elves*. San Diego, Calif.: Harcourt Brace Jovanovich, 1991.

Robbins, Ruth. *Baboushka and the Three Kings*. Illustrated by Nicolas Sidjakov. New York: Parnassus Press, 1960.

Watts, Bernadette. *The Elves and the Shoemaker*. New York: North-South Books, 1986.

Whitney, Thomas P., trans. *Vasilisa the Beautiful*. Illustrated by Nonny Hogrogian. New York: Macmillan, 1970.

Willard, Nancy. *Beauty and the Beast*. Illustrated by Barry Moser. New York: Harcourt Brace Jovanovich, 1992.

Young, Ed. *Lon Po Po: A Red-Riding Hood Story from China*. New York: Philomel Books, 1989.

Magazines

National Geographic. monthly.

Yankee. monthly.

The Basics

What makes up a story? What makes up a piece of music? Every art form has its elements. Like a tantalizing cake whose flavors combine into an unforgettable taste experience, a work of art consists of separate ingredients, that, when brought together with aesthetic vision, result in a wonderful, finished piece.

Chapter 2 includes activities that examine the individual elements of stories and music to better understand how parts work within a whole piece. Although this analysis explores traditional elements that can be defined and examined separately according to guidelines or rules, the chemistry of any artwork is elusive. Both creator and receiver contribute to the total experience.

Each storytelling or music activity will help you and your students discover the individual ingredients needed for each art form. The collaborative activities are designed to be simple explorations combining stories and music in an easy, guided way. Armed with a better understanding of the elements, students can move confidently into chapter 3, "Putting It All Together: Organization and Structure."

THE BASICS OF STORIES

As the *events* of a narrative unfold, *characters* move through the *landscape* of a story, and out of their actions and behavior, the story's *themes* arise. The literary elements explored in this chapter are plot, character, setting, and theme.

Each element will be defined and discussed in the following sections, with age-appropriate activities suggested to enhance students' understanding of these elements basic to stories. By focusing on how each part works in simple folktales, younger students will become more comfortable playing with story parts as they prepare to compose their own narratives. For students in grades four through six, this recognition will help prepare them for understanding more complex works of literature, even as it also aids their composing process. It is important to remember that, although we can look closely at each element, no part of a story is completely separate from the others. Characters' actions depend not only on who they are but on where they are. A setting can determine how one acts. Themes emerge naturally from a story's events. With this in mind, the best we can do is recognize that narrative has identifiable aspects, each with certain qualities and a job to do.

Only these four elements—plot, character, setting, theme—were chosen from a longer list of possibilities for several reasons. This book is not an exhaustive, technical study of all story and musical elements, only an introduction to those parts basic to an understanding of how the art forms work. Certainly *style, tone,* and *mood* are legitimate areas of inquiry, but they seem too subtle for our purposes. *Point of view* is frequently analyzed in children's literature, and you should feel free to explore it. The most common activity for this is to retell a story from another character's point of view, an engaging and revealing exploration. It might not be worthwhile here to advance activities beyond that—we want to engage students, not disenchant them. Here, less is indeed more.

Plot

Plot, as we know, is the sequence of events—what happens in a story. It is certainly easy enough to identify events, but we may overlook the significance of how they are arranged in terms of helping students understand how stories work. In folktales, as in authored stories, events usually follow some type of logical order: The Little Red Hen finds her seeds and plants them; the wheat grows and is made into a loaf of bread. The fisherman's wife wishes for a sequence of increasingly impressive dwellings, with a matching role for herself. In "The Turnip" (Domanska), one by one, family members join the tugging line. Often in folklore, the main character must journey to far-off places to fulfill tasks of increasing difficulty or find a precious object. Thus, a folktale plot may happen in one small barnyard or may develop from here to the home of the North Wind and back, but there is always some kind of connection between events.

For younger students, ages 5-7, enhancing awareness of a simple sequence is appropriate, as is identifying a problem (conflict) to be solved. Through increasingly challenging activities, students aged 8-12 may identify and invent story events with more complex connections. The concept of cause and effect, for example, is basic to all fiction. Engaging older students in interesting explorations of causal connections in stories can provide a background for their later encounters with Shakespeare's plays and young adult novels. They will also benefit from recognizing four basic types of conflict inherent in narrative: person against person: person against society; person against nature; and person against self.

The one activity suggested for younger students in this chapter is "Walking with Rosie," meant to be generic for simple plot sequences. Other story structures are explored in chapter 3 as more holistic story experiences.

Walking with Rosie

Concepts: Enhancing a sense of story structure.

Materials: *Rosie's Walk* (Hutchins), rectangular felt board at least 2 feet long, felt pieces of each site and object mentioned in the story (rake, pond, haystack, etc.), seven felt silhouettes of Rosie and seven of the fox.

Ages: 5-7.

The activities in "Walking with Rosie" are not particularly innovative. The idea is to reinforce the concept of story structure with ongoing visual, tactile, listening, reading, and oral experiences. It is hoped that primary-level teachers will use this approach to the wealth of stories appealing to their students.

1. Read or tell the story with the illustrations. (The fox is never mentioned in the text.) Take your time and have fun with each of the fox's accidents.

2. Present the felt board either blank or with the sites in place. As you retell the story, students place the appropriate objects, a Rosie and a fox for each event, beginning with Rosie starting her walk with the fox lurking behind. For each event, there will be a Rosie and a fox, ending with the fox chased "over the hill and far away," and Rosie returning home.

3. Retell the story again, with all objects in place.

4. Use these follow-up activities for other days:

   • Scramble the event sites on the felt board, keeping the first and last in place, then retell the story. Will students correct you? Except for the opening and the ending chase, the sequence is purely arbitrary—the central events could happen in any order. Students' insistence on the authority of the text, however, is a valuable insight that this is a work of art, and that our experience of the story is as much due to the author's vision as to our response.

   • Place the felt board at a learning center where students may retell the story to themselves or others (parents, aides, classmates), either by placing the felt pieces on the board or following the pieces already in place. Or, students may follow the story on tape, told by the teacher, a classmate, or themselves, as they place or observe the felt pieces.

   • Invent new episodes for *Rosie's Walk*, prepare felt pieces, and retell the story. For an entirely new story, make a class book with the felt pieces or other cutouts and present to the school library. Three or four books later, you will have an interesting collection of Rosie stories.

   • *Rosie's Walk* is perfect for classroom drama for ages 7 and 8. Give second- and third-graders the responsibility of identifying the events and spacing out the action sites. Students themselves can be the rake, the haystack, the pond, and so on. The teacher's guiding hand moves Rosie and the fox through the perilous sites to a satisfying conclusion. The production may be scored with various rhythm instruments. Students decide which sound is most effective for each event.

   • See chapter 4 for the activity "Rosie Revisited," which is based on this same picture book.

Fences

Concepts: Developing an understanding of conflict in narrative.

Materials: One or more of these books: *How Many Spots Does a Leopard Have?* (Lester), *The Man Who Could Call Down Owls* (Bunting), *How the Stars Fell into the Sky: A Navajo Legend* (Oughton), *When Moose Was Young* (Latimer), *The Land of Gray Wolf* (Locker); mural paper for classroom or hall display; sheets of tagboard or foam core; a variety of art papers, crayons, markers, paint, colored pencils, glue, and scissors or craft knives.

Ages: 10-12.

This activity is a visual representation of several types of conflict commonly found in literature. It can be easily combined with character exploration, if desired. The display may take any form appropriate for your class and may be a one-time exercise or added to over several weeks. The books listed are suggestions. Any story with a well-defined conflict will work.

1. From the tagboard or foam core, construct several sizes of picket fences (high, low, long, short) by spacing and gluing pointed verticals across horizontal strips as samples for students' constructions. The picket fence design allows more of a character (or less, depending on the size of the fence) to be seen and will provide a desirable three-dimensional effect.

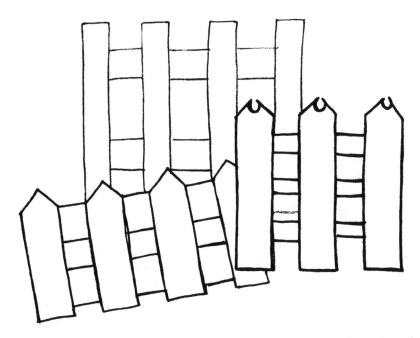

2. For each story read (whole class, small groups, or individually), identify and discuss the conflicts and the characters or forces involved.

3. One or more students may construct a fence (let students choose the size) and some type of visual representation of the characters or forces in conflict. Because this is not meant primarily as an art lesson, shapes may be simple, even abstract (a black oval for an owl).

4. Place the opposing characters on opposite sides of the fence, either facing or turned away. The fence should predominate between them. The grouping is mounted on any background you prefer: a hall display, a room mural, a frieze, a mini-display at a learning center. Identify each grouping by story title, author, characters' names, or forces' names. Discuss with students how to represent multiple conflicts in one story (one fence or several?).

5. A variation: For stories in which conflict is resolved, at one end of the fence add a gate carrying a few words (a line of dialogue, a descriptive phrase) that represent the resolution.

6. Periodically review your fence display, comparing and contrasting stories with similar or different types of conflict. Characterization may be included by indicating on the display various qualities of the characters that may have contributed to the conflict or its resolution (foolishness, wisdom, greed, pride, etc.). When you begin to see qualities repeated among the groups, you might color code them to visually reinforce students' sense that story characters often display common human failings and virtues, particularly in folklore, and that these are integral to the plot.

Character

To explore story characters, we consider their behavior in various situations and settings, what they say and think, and how they talk, as well as what other characters say and think about them. All of these are conventional choices available to writers to develop characterization. Recognizing and exploring these choices in folklore will prepare students to do the same in authored stories.

Folklore characters are defined as one-dimensional, undeveloped stereotypes. In one sense, this is true. Some characters will forever play tricks; some characters are cast for their unique roles from the beginning. Conversely, these flat characters often exhibit either admirable qualities of great courage, imagination, wit, and caring, or obviously undesirable traits such as greed, pride, selfishness, and evil intent.

Medieval morality plays powerfully conveyed the message of good triumphant and evil overthrown (the common theme in folklore) through flat, allegorical figures who nonetheless had humor and personality. Just as twelfth-century audiences responded to a cunning trickster Devil, a boisterous goodwife, or an innocent Everyman, so students will respond to an exploration of folklore characters to enhance awareness of how all characters function in any story.

Remembering that it is impossible to completely separate character from other story elements of plot, setting, and theme, the following activities are designed to shine a light on characterization: how we experience and come to know a particular person in a story. Younger children (ages 5-7) are encouraged to look at individual characters; intermediate and older children (ages 8-12) are more capable of considering not only individual characteristics but the interaction between characters.

The first two activities have been developed from *The Legend of Sleepy Hollow* by Washington Irving and are meant to be examples of a general approach to characterization. For folktales where description may be absent, discuss with students, before the activity, story characters' probable physical qualities: their posture, walk, use of hands, facial expression, and so on, based on how we perceive them in the story. Ask students to write a brief description of these characters, incorporating their ideas, and perhaps Irving's descriptions, quoted below, as models. Use these invented descriptions as movement starters, as suggested below.

Finding the Shape

Concepts: Discovering and exploring a character's essential qualities.

Materials: *The Legend of Sleepy Hollow* (Irving, illustrated by Van Nutt).

Ages: 7-12, with variations as noted.

This book is available by itself or with an audiocassette narrated by Glenn Close, with music by Tim Story. The illustrations by Van Nutt very nicely show the characters' body shapes as described by Irving. The original story first appeared in Irving's *The Sketch Book*.

1. Read the story to the class, showing the illustrations and commenting on the physical appearance of Ichabod, Katrina, and Brom Bones. In Irving's original story, he describes Ichabod as looking like a "crane"; Katrina as a "plump little partridge"; and Brom Bones as "burly, roaring, roistering."

2. Standing in an open space, have the class try imitating body shapes of a crane (long legs and neck stretched out); a partridge (small, plump, fast-moving); and a bear (heavy, thick, lumbering). You may wish to use pictures of these creatures for visual reinforcement. Students are not to move around, simply experiment with the body conformations in their individual spaces.

3. Now take the imaginative step from animal to person. Read the following descriptions of the three main characters, pointing out how Irving describes them as persons but with many animal or bird qualities. (Irving does not call Brom Bones a "bear," but this seems a reasonable animal to use, given Bones's description.) As you slowly read the descriptions, ask students to add each physical aspect while remaining in their spaces. They will need to "think" some aspects, such as "huge ears" or "rosy-cheeked."

Ichabod: "He was tall, but exceedingly lank, with narrow shoulders, long arms and legs, hands that dangled a mile out of his sleeves, feet that might have served for shovels, and his whole frame was loosely hung together. His head was small and flat at top, with huge ears, large green glassy eyes, and a long snipe nose . . . perched upon his spindle neck. To see him striding along . . . with his clothes bagging and fluttering about him, one might have mistaken him for . . . some scarecrow."

To avoid stiff, unnatural positions, explain and emphasize "lank" and loose-limbed. Ichabod is all knees and joints. Take another look at the book illustrations.

Katrina: "She was a blooming lass of fresh eighteen; plump as a partridge; ripe and melting and rosy-cheeked as one of her father's peaches . . . a little of a coquette . . . and a provokingly short petticoat, to display the prettiest foot and ankle in the country round."

"Flirt" explains "coquette" for students, and that is exactly what Katrina is. The easiest way to transform a plump partridge shape into Katrina is to flutter fingers (as if bird wings) and eyelashes and turn one foot out to show a pretty ankle. Boys of all ages make wonderful Katrinas; encourage them—demonstrate that you are all working on the essential qualities of a particular character, not a stereotyped idea of girlish flirting. Avoid an overly simpering caricature: Katrina is a simple country girl who likes to dance, not a doll.

Brom Bones: "A burly, roaring, roistering blade . . . the hero of the country round . . . broad-shouldered, with a mingled air of fun and arrogance . . . famed for great knowledge and skill in horsemanship . . . always ready for either a fight or a frolic; but had more mischief than ill-will in his composition."

It is crucial to emphasize that Brom is not mean-spirited or dangerous, but someone whose idea of fun is physical action: horsemanship and harmless scuffling. His heavy, thick shape contrasts nicely with Katrina's roundness and Ichabod's bony joints. By focusing on each character's "center of power," the shapes may come more easily. Katrina's may be in her ankle ("the prettiest ankle, etc."); Ichabod's in his head (the schoolmaster); and Brom Bones's in his shoulders and chest (the horseman).

4. When the class is comfortable with each character's overall shape, have everyone move randomly in their space, first as Ichabod, then as Katrina, then as Brom, maintaining several body characteristics for each one. Playing a different rhythm instrument for each character will help to maintain individual qualities. Try wood blocks for Ichabod—they sound "bony." A bell sound for Katrina adds to her lightness—a glockenspiel, wind chimes, or a tambourine, for example. Brom moves well to a drum. Vary the beat so that movement does not become marching.

5. Divide the class into thirds, and assign a character to each group. All students will move simultaneously around the space as one of the three characters. This time, give each character a phrase to say as they meet and pass the others.

Ichabod: "I'm the new schoolmaster."

Katrina: "I'm the prettiest girl in town."

Brom Bones: "I'm the hero of the countryside."

Try this in slow motion as well as normal movement, with an occasional "freeze" during which students observe their classmates and describe what they see.

Shadow Theatre

Concepts: Enhancing awareness of a character's essential qualities.

Materials: A white bed sheet (double or larger), overhead projector or spot-
light, teacher aide or other adult to help with this activity.

Ages: 7-12.

Just as for the previous activity, "Finding the Shape," this activity can easily be adapted to any desired story by identifying key physical qualities of a story's characters. Think about arm and leg shapes, head and hand positions, shoulders—the body parts that can easily be recognized in a silhouette.

1. To set up a shadow theatre, the sheet may be hung from an overhead rope or wire or (perhaps easier) pinned between the inner edges of a stage curtain. The curtain is opened to stretch the sheet taut. Try to eliminate wrinkles. The light source should be at least 10 to 12 feet behind the sheet so that the whole sheet surface is lit. An overhead projector works well.

2. Seat the class on the floor in front of the sheet, at least 6 feet away. One adult stays with the class; another is behind the sheet. Three students at a time take their places behind the sheet, each assuming the shape of one of the characters: Ichabod, Katrina, or Brom, as they have experienced them in the previous activity, "Finding the Shape." Students choose their shape in secret after coming behind the sheet.

3. Help students to assume their shapes so that their silhouettes show each character's outline. For example, Ichabod should show elbows and knees, Katrina her ankle or fluttery fingers, Brom his shoulders. For crisp outlines, students must be as close to the sheet as possible, without overlapping. They hold the position in a freeze.

4. With the help of the adult in front, the class guesses each character. Avoid identifying classmates by name. Look for the character and ask students to describe what they see. In this way, they are focusing on the shape, which suggests personality traits, without the distraction of faces, colors, clothing, and so on.

5. Repeat until all students have participated, varying the placement and outline of each character with each group. Conclude with a wrap-up discussion of the three characters as portrayed in the story. You may refer to book illustrations, but the idea is not to replicate the artist's vision as the only one way to portray the characters, but to dig into the text and discover the writer's characterizations, based on evidence in the text.

Outside In

Concepts: Enhancing understanding of a character's essential qualities.

Materials: Any story the class wants to explore, *The Jolly Postman: Or Other People's Letters* (Ahlbergs), a variety of writing and art materials (see below).

Ages: 7-12.

Each of these activities is a way of considering a character from the outside, rather than from within, as in the previous two activities. The activities allow students to extend their vision of how a character may behave, think, or respond within the story context. Again, conclusions must be reasonably based on what we know from the text. The range of possibilities, however, in any one activity (or several combined) is generous enough to add dimension to the character. Each activity is stated as a question and may be pursued in various forms: improvisational drama, art projects, audiotape or videotape, or simply discussion.

1. For any character in any story the class wants to explore, have students consider what other characters might be saying about him or her:

    Two neighbors walking home from choir practice?

    Two classmates walking home from school?

    Two gossips with time to spare?

    Emphasize that not all conversations should be negative or "gossip" in the worst sense. This is also one way to focus on a particular story event.

2. What kind of mail might be found in this character's mailbox? To lead into this activity, share with the class *The Jolly Postman*. Note the various types of mail in this book; discuss possibilities and create imaginative mail for your character. How might some of this mail advance or change the story's plot?

3. What would this character store in boxes or barrels in the attic or basement? A classroom box might hold a collection of likely items placed there by students. A whole class discussion focuses on each item's significance for the character. Several not-so-likely-but-possible items placed by the teacher will enhance critical thinking.

These last two ideas can be extended to many aspects of everyday life. What movies, TV shows, or music might this character like? If this character were a new student in the class, what would your welcome be? What field trip would this character like, and how might this person behave?

4. What would this character's room look like? Design a contemporary bedroom or playroom for this character, including furniture, posters, books, stereo equipment, games—whatever seems appropriate. You may, of course, research furnishings and appropriate items of the period. Designs should include clothing and ways to store it. This project may be done individually or as a class display, as drawings or as a miniature set design. (See the activity "Setting the Stage," later in this chapter.) For a single display, perhaps in the library, add a tape recorder with your choice of appropriate music to be played by viewers.

This last activity overlaps with the element of setting but is meant to illuminate story characters, their personal lives, and traits that are not specified in the text. You will want to begin with any information in the story about a room or dwelling, then add details appropriate to the text.

Setting

The setting of a story is usually not identified as a separate literary element, at least not a crucial one. It somehow ends up allied with plot. However, a story's setting, which includes not only time and place but also weather, seasons, interiors, and exteriors, can be as critical as plot or characterization in the story experience.

Although the conventional settings in folklore—woods, cottage, castle, cave, or mountain—are endlessly replicated like paper cutouts throughout the folklore canon, each type of setting holds rich possibilities for exploration kinesthetically and aurally. What does the warmth or chill of this place have to do with a character's behavior? How do light and darkness affect this scene? What are the sounds and silences in this forest? How do this story's landscapes reveal the themes? These questions can guide teachers' and students' investigation of setting.

As with previous activities in this chapter for other literary elements, the following are designed as general approaches to exploring setting and will work as well for authored stories as for folktales. Those specifically for younger students are not intended to teach setting as a concept, merely to heighten awareness of landscape or weather.

All Kinds of Weather

Concepts: Discovering the importance of weather as a story element.

Materials: Suggested books: *Cloudy with a Chance of Meatballs* (Barrett), *Waiting-for-Spring Stories* (Roberts), *Waiting-for-Papa Stories* (Roberts), *The Three Bears & 15 Other Stories* (Rockwell); various art supplies; felt board with figures (see below).

Ages: 5-7.

Exploring how weather functions as part of a story's setting can be connected to science lessons in weather. This activity also combines well with a unit on nutrition. Have students imagine the most- and least-nutritional meals that could fall from the sky. Students may write their own version of this story in writing, with illustrations.

1. *Cloudy with a Chance of Meatballs* is a wonderfully improbable picture book in which the town's inhabitants receive their food each day from the sky. What they eat depends on weather conditions, and when the weather turns nasty, so does the food. This story tells so well, it is worth the effort to learn it so that the class can hear it without the book illustrations. Their own mental imagery is then the basis for drawings or a class art project representing both the "normal" foodfall and the storm. The teacher should lead students on a walk around the classroom as though they were walking through the town in the story. Students encounter imaginary puddles of catsup (thick and slushy) and syrup (thinner but sticky) while dodging pancakes, meatballs, and large rolls.

2. Several stories in *Waiting-for-Spring Stories* are ideal for drama in "Story Theatre" form, with a narrator and characters playing out the action. "Story Theatre" is drama in which characters mime the action without dialogue (or with very little dialogue) as a narrator reads from a script (or recites the script from memory). The stories in *Waiting-for-Spring Stories* involve seasonal changes as well as weather. Also see *Waiting-for-Papa Stories*.

3. "The Star Money," in *The Three Bears & 15 Other Stories*, is about a child who gives away her clothing to each cold, shivering person she meets. As day ends and night comes on, she enters the woods, cold and dark, where her predicament is solved by the star money. Use a felt board to retell this story, changing the colors of people, objects, and the landscape from light to dark to visually convey the changing setting and ending with the bright, warm, comforting star money.

Into the Woods

Concepts: Exploring the "wood" as a classic story setting.

Materials: A variety of rhythm instruments, two or three long scarves in dark colors.

Ages: 6-12, with age-appropriate modifications.

This activity has been widely classroom-tested in first through sixth grades, and it never fails. The process is incremental, and it is important not to skip the preliminaries or rush the sequence. The following explanation is for fourth grade and up, but even six-year-olds can form an impressive wood by simplifying the forming of "trees" and adding fewer and simpler sounds.

1. In an open area large enough for each student to have their own space, ask the class to show you a tree. Students will probably raise both arms as limbs. Ask the class to review pictures or look out a window at whatever trees are visible and note the wide variety of branch shapes and the angles of limbs.

2. With students again in their own spaces, ask them to discover how many angles they can make with body parts in isolation: first the head, then just the shoulders, proceeding to arms (including hands and fingers), then the waist, legs and feet, each part explored separately. This becomes an amazing discovery of possibilities. Be sure students understand what an angle is. For this activity, an angle can be described as "the bending of a straight line." Demonstrate by bending your straightened arm at the elbow.

3. Again ask students to form a tree, knowing now how many angles their bodies own. Basic rules: both feet flat on the floor, and the position must be one the student can hold comfortably for a few minutes.

4. Next, the teacher groups "trees" into an interesting wood, avoiding long, open aisles. Several students may join "branches"; several may be bushes to add variety in height. The class has now created a generic wood, available for exploration, according to any particular story.

Add each of the following steps in sequence, building to the final effect.

5. Students drop their poses but stay in place for a discussion of appropriate woodland sounds: various birds, small night sounds, the wind, creaking of branches, for example. Designate one or two students for each sound. Resume poses and experiment with sounds. At this point, you may wish to lower the lights. Add each sound one by one, slowly and quietly, gradually building to the final effect, which should be soft and random. Tree branches may sway gently in the wind. Two or three scarves may be draped on branches throughout the wood.

6. The next step is to "orchestrate" your wood to enhance the woodland sounds. Several students can experiment with single sounds on various rhythm instruments. Wind chimes, finger cymbals, a drumbeat, a guiro rasp, for example, add variety, particularly when students are positioned around the wood's edges. Introduce these sounds randomly, and keep them soft. Remember, less is more. Keep it simple.

7. Your wood is now ready for story characters to enter and explore for one scene. Characters should either be silent or invent one appropriate vocal sound. If there is a ghost, as in Washington Irving's *The Legend of Sleepy Hollow*, a shiver is effective. Keep it soft. The wood in *The Wind in the Willows*, by Kenneth Grahame, is cold and snowy with unidentified scurryings. Woods in folktales may be sheltering and friendly places where animals roam freely, or they may be menacing places where trees block the way. If your story includes animals, ask them to find their home in the wood—a hole, bush, burrow, and so on. Direct characters to move in slow motion to avoid rushing through this setting. All students will be involved in creating a living, exciting setting that will encourage improvisation and discovery within a story.

8. After the scene, have everyone sit down where they are and discuss how they felt about their actions. Were the trees pleased to be able to help a lost animal? How did a homeless ghost feel with no shelter? Did the sounds add to a wanderer's fear? Did anything startling happen? Anything unexpected? Discuss how these events enhance the story.

9. Variation for ages 9 and up: In many stories, the wood literally inhibits one or more characters from continuing. To dramatically explore this situation, give conflicting instructions to the wood and to characters involved. For example, Mole, from *The Wind in the Willows*, is lost in a snowstorm in the Wild Wood, hunting for Badger's house. Out of hearing-range of the class, tell Mole that, *no matter what happens*, his objective is to find shelter, out of the storm, under a tree or behind a bush, for example. The student should be motivated and know what to look for. Then, out of Mole's hearing, tell the various trees, bushes, and so on to impede his progress. The trees turn their backs to him; bushes curl up; all elements close him out quite clearly. Send Mole into the woods. Ideally, he should become so frantic that he just gives up in frustration. Everyone experiences what it would be like for a small animal to be lost in a dark, cold, unfriendly wood. Stop the action, sit down, and talk about how Mole and the wood felt. The "trees" frequently say, "I felt good, shutting him out." The question is, "Why?" Students will usually be willing to explore this reaction more seriously. The results may, if desired, be applied to classroom or other school situations. The immediate focus, however, is intended to be on the story.

This approach, setting up an improvisational conflict, is a highly effective, creative drama activity, as students are faced with the unexpected and must find ways to improvise. It also works well when exploring plot.

Setting the Stage

Concepts: Enhancing understanding of how setting functions in a story.

Materials: Any story the class wants to explore; various art materials: tag-
        board or foam core, index cards, drawing paper, crayons, markers,
        colored pencils, glue, and scissors.

Ages: 5-12.

The basic activity is to design a setting for one episode in a story. Students' ages determine the complexity of the format.

1. With younger students (ages 5-7), discuss a particular setting (e.g., barnyard, cottage, a wood, seashore) and the action of the story in that setting. Each student draws their own vision of this scene without reference to book illustrations. Discuss the variety of drawings. Each will be individual in arrangement, size of objects, and interpretation of the landscape. Encourage students to acknowledge the validity of each vision—each mind's eye sees this scene somewhat differently. Simple folktales with little description work well for this activity.

2. Next, compare the same object in several of these drawings. It should be an object that varies in size, shape, color, and so on—a tree or house, for example. Discuss with students what the characters might feel like in relation to this object. What they might say, or how they might walk, for instance. Could you take a nap under this big tree? Would you like to slide down this haystack? What color curtains would you hang at this window? Retell the particular story scene, adding the new details in a fashion appropriate for the class, such as creative drama or added dialogue, for example.

3. Older students (ages 8-12) may design a miniature stage set for a story scene. Use a piece of tagboard or foam core, 18 to 20 inches long by 8 to 9 inches wide. Score it according to the diagram below to make a simple, three-sided set.

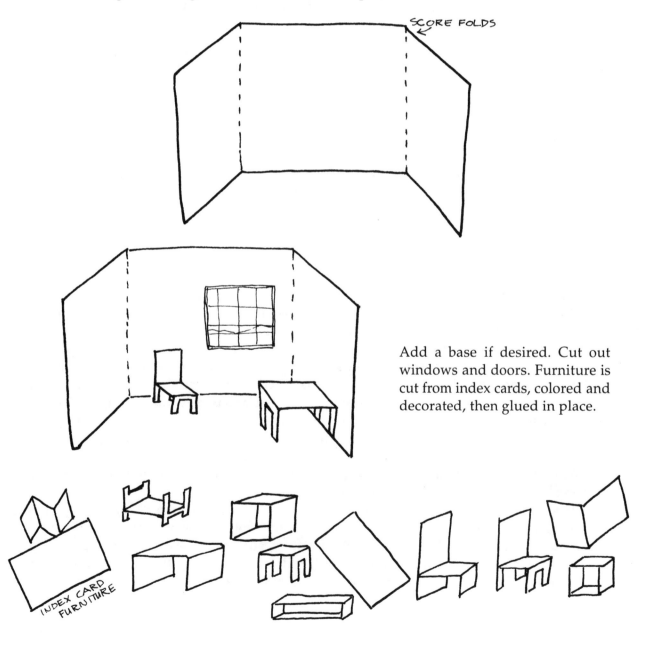

Add a base if desired. Cut out windows and doors. Furniture is cut from index cards, colored and decorated, then glued in place.

Landscapes may be created from tissue paper, fabrics, cellophane, or natural materials. Play with textures, colors, and shapes. A thin wire or cord stretched from side to side across the top of the set allows objects to hang freely, to float in space.

Encourage the use of detail so that students may explore this setting more fully.

4. This project may also be done individually or collaboratively in small groups. Ask students to discuss their conceptions with the class, talking about how colors, shapes, and so on might influence characters' actions in the story.

Theme

As characters move through the landscapes and adventures of their story, as event follows event, a theme emerges: a central idea, a reason beyond pure pleasure for the story's existence. In folklore, the primary theme of good over evil is revealed by the actions and values of sympathetic characters with whom people can identify. Courage, kindness, cleverness, wit, a sense of purpose, friendship, and an awareness of the needs of others are qualities common in folktales. Students gain a conviction that even the youngest and most ignored daughter or son can triumph through goodness and perseverance. Magic? Yes, but remember that only those judged worthy are presented with magic objects or powers to ease their way. Conversely, antagonists are clearly identified by their greed, anger, selfishness, and lust for power or money, and they are frequently short-sighted.

As theme is the most abstract literary element, the following activities are suitable for students aged 9 and up. Primary students can be encouraged to recognize characters' qualities without attempting to formulate a complete theme statement for a story. It is important to remember that theme statements are not "morals," as in fables. The theme is the expression of one of the central ideas of a story, such as, "They tried, they lied, they failed." In well-written literature (including children's literature), themes are seldom, if ever, directly stated but must be inferred.

The Great Lie

Concepts: Exploring the act of lying as a thematic idea in stories.

Materials: *The Rough-Face Girl* (Martin), three rocks (the more interesting in shape and texture, the better).

Ages: 9-12.

Lying, whether for good or ill, is a fairly common occurrence in both authored stories and folklore. This activity allows students to explore both the act of lying and their feelings about it. In *The Rough-Face Girl*, for example, the two older sisters lie in hopes of becoming the Invisible Being's bride and, of course, fail. Martin's story is worded for girls, but this activity would work equally well for any story or book in which lying is a key factor. The process works best with minimal or no explanation.

1. Ask for three volunteers, or choose three students to help demonstrate one of this story's themes through an improvised drama.

2. Place rocks on the floor in plain sight of the class. Explain that, on the day the rough-face girl's great-grandmother was born, a magic rock fell from the skies, and that this rock has assured safety and happiness to the women of her family over the generations, through risks and dangers. The rock, however, was lost some time ago. Three rocks have been found, one of which is the magic rock; only the daughter with truth in her heart will know beyond doubt which is the magic rock. You may say something like, "I'm sure each of you wants us to believe that your rock is the true rock, but at least two of you will be lying and will know in your heart that your words are untrue."

3. Each of the three students chooses a rock and defends her choice verbally. The teacher and class may ask questions, if they wish. You may want to set a time limit.

4. After all three have defended their choices, the class evaluates how convincing each argument was. The point is not only to decide which is the true rock, but more important, to assess the act of lying. How do you feel when you lie? Does your body betray you? Your eyes, voice? Is it okay to lie in certain circumstances? In this activity, all three could be lying.

I Wish, I Wish!

Concepts: Enabling students to explore an archetypal literary theme.

Materials: *The Fisherman and His Wife* (Stewig), *The Stonecutter* (McDermott), paper stars 4-5 inches wide, paper circles 3-4 inches in diameter, markers, glue, a piece of tagboard or construction paper, 20 by 24 inches, for each group.

Ages: 9-12.

A familiar theme in literature (including children's literature) is the danger of getting what you wish for. Read or tell several folktales with this theme, such as *The Fisherman and His Wife* or *The Stonecutter*.

1. The whole class brainstorms a list of wishes: to be very rich, to be king or queen, to live forever, to be invisible, and so forth. Post the list for students' reference.

2. Students work collaboratively in small groups. Each group chooses a wish from the list or composes a new one. Try for variety, so that each group is working with a different wish. Each group should have a piece of tagboard or construction paper, a paper star, five or six paper circles, and glue.

3. Each group's scribe writes the selected wish on the paper star and glues it in the center of the tagboard. The group then brainstorms possible consequences for the wish, recording them on paper circles.

4. Glue the circles in a pattern around the star, connecting each circle to the star with a line. If any connections are perceived between consequences, indicate this with a line drawn between circles. Students may wish to indicate in some way which results they perceive as major, perhaps with a differently colored circle or marker.

5. Share group results with the class, noting similar or identical consequences. Discussions growing out of this sharing may spread over several days.

6. As a visual representation of this activity, mount a classroom or hall display in a webbing format, in which similar consequences for different wishes are joined or overlapped. Embellish the display with student artwork of wishes and consequences. Student illustrations for stories read in connection with this activity may also go on the display.

7. As the class encounters authored books with this theme, repeat the activity or simply discuss wishes and consequences. Remember that a wish does not have to be phrased, "I wish for . . ." It may be what a character desires to have or to be.

THE BASICS OF MUSIC

Music is the art form that children understand and become involved with earliest; however, not being able to see music makes it more challenging for students to verbalize what music is. Babies absorb sound, speech, and music even before they are born, as hearing develops in the fetus around the sixth month of pregnancy. Before children can read, they are singing and moving. Also, young students are not prejudiced against certain kinds of music. They like any kind of music, especially if it is lively and rhythmic. Music soothes people when they are restless, irritable, or overextended.

In its simplest definition, music is organized sound. Sound that occurs naturally is not music, but these sounds can become music if they are organized in some fashion.

In this section, we will be discovering sounds and exploring the elements of music. Each of these concepts will have several exploratory activities to involve students. The collaborative part of the chapter will bring together concepts explored individually to create pieces using both music and stories.

Discovering Body Sounds

Body sounds are useful in working with music. Body sounds were mentioned in the introduction as a source for music making. The following activities will help teachers discover the many possibilities of body sounds. Once you realize all the ways that bodies can make sounds, you can use them in other activities in this book.

There are two basic types of sounds that can be created with the body:

Wind sounds use breath. They include whistling, singing, humming, throat sounds, and other mouth sounds. Make a list of all possible sounds that use breath and then create symbols for these sounds. This will help when you begin to organize sounds in compositions and you need to notate the sounds. Use symbols that best describe the character of the sound. For example:

WHISTLING   CLAPPING   TONGUE CLICKS   "OOOOO"

Percussive sounds occur when the body is struck or hit in some way. Examples include patting knees, clapping hands, clicking the tongue, and stomping feet. There are a multitude of possibilities. Chart these sounds and create symbols representing each sound.

Sounds to Me Like . . .

Concepts: Finding ways to make sounds.

Materials: Screen big enough to hide a student.

Ages: 6 and up.

These simple activities can be done whenever you have a few minutes to spare. They are a good way for students to have fun in a productive way.

1. Each student finds their own sound. Play a guessing game by having a student hide behind a screen and make the sound while the class tries to guess how the sound is made.

2. A student or small group uses one body sound and performs a familiar tune. Class guesses the tune.

3. Play Simon Says. The person who is "it" makes one sound; the class repeats the sound. Continue adding body sounds one at a time, with the same person as "it" or each student adding another sound.

4. For older students: Assign small groups, giving each group one of the following situations. They are to use only the sounds given, not words. Encourage students to limit use of body language.

   - Using only vowel sounds, describe the weather.

   - Using the syllable "la," persuade your teacher that your dog ate your homework.

   - Using gibberish, explain to your mom why you didn't clean your room.

   - Using only tongue clicks, describe a ride at an amusement park.

Think of other relevant situations for your students. Limit sounds to specific vowels, consonants, mouth sounds, or gibberish. Students should practice and then perform for the class. Class guesses what the situation is. Evaluate. What in the improvisation helped reveal to the class what the situation was? How about the tone, repetition, volume, speed? This exercise will also serve as a good introduction to musical controls and elements.

Sounds Around Us

One exciting aspect of twentieth-century music is its use of everyday, ordinary sounds in musical composition. Composers have discovered how to use sounds around us in their natural existence ("*musique concrète*" or "found" sounds) and how to manipulate them to create new musical sounds. Concurrently, the proliferation of electronics in the music industry presents unlimited possibilities for exploring sounds using keyboard synthesizers and other electronic instruments. Today computers and synthesizers are used frequently in pop, commercial, and classical music. The following activities deal with sounds that exist around us and offer ways to tap their potential for music making.

This is a simple exercise for all ages. Have students close their eyes for thirty seconds or one minute. All they are to do is listen. After the time is up, ask them what they heard. They should have heard many sounds that exist normally but that we automatically shut out. The purpose is to point out the variety of sounds around us. It is difficult to find an environment that is truly silent. Also, the many kinds of sounds around us are really fascinating. After all, we are made with eyelids but not "ear lids." What does that tell us about the importance of listening? The exercises that follow are also "earobic."

A Sound Scavenger Hunt

Concepts: Becoming more sensitive to the sounds around us.

Materials: List of sounds.

Ages: 10 and up.

Instead of the usual scavenger hunt to find unusual things, your students will look for unusual sounds.

1. Decide where your scavenger hunt will be. Compile a list of sounds to discover. Here are some sounds to find:

a crunchy sound	a funny sound
an absolutely awful sound	a soothing sound
a sound that whistles	a metallic sound
a sound you have never noticed before	a two-click sound
a sound that reminds you of a lemon	a quiet sound
a sound that occurs over your head	a shaking sound
a sound found below your knees	a sound using water
a blowing sound	a hitting sound
the loudest sound you hear	an irritating sound

2. Variation: Each student writes down all the sounds heard in one room of their house. Class tries to guess what room it is.

The Environmental Orchestra

Concepts: Classifying sounds.

Materials: Possible objects for sounds.

Ages: 10 and up.

In a traditional orchestra, musical instruments are divided into "families" with common properties unique to each family: strings, woodwinds, brass, and percussion. Each family of instruments creates vibrations that cause them to sound in similar fashion:

strings—plucking or bowing strings

woodwinds—blowing air through a column

brass—vibrating air through the lips (embouchure), amplifying through a mouthpiece and instrument

percussion—hitting, striking, or shaking instrument

These methods of sound production determine the family they belong to. As with real families, many variations within each instrumental family can be found—size, material, quality, and complexity, to name a few.

In the environmentally correct chamber orchestra, "ECCO" for short, the sounds are recycled from the world around us—objects, sounds with other primary meanings, and sounds our bodies make. As with families of instruments in a traditional orchestra, the found instruments of the "environmental orchestra" can be organized into families.

1. To assemble an ECCO, first determine the families you want to have and how the sounds will be related. For instance, you might call the families: human, animal, environmental, and man-made materials. (These are the families of sounds used in the collaborative activity "ECCO Meets Jack—A Sound Story," found later in this chapter.)

2. Students are divided into four groups and given their family name. They find appropriate sounds to fit into their family. The human sounds could be laughing, patting, clapping, and any body or mouth percussion sounds. The animal sounds could be braying, hoof beats, meowing, barking, growling. The environmental sounds are made from nature: leaves crunching, ocean waves, rain, thunder, wind. The man-made sounds include paper rustling, keys shaking, and a book falling.

3. Once students have an assortment of sounds for their musical family, they can improvise a concert.

    a. First, seat students in an orchestra-like arrangement.

    b. Choose a conductor to lead the performers with hand and other nonverbal gestures. The quality, strength, and speed of the conductor's body expressions give the performers information on how they should perform their sounds.

    c. The conductor directs the families, using gestures. The music should be spontaneous and improvised, just following the conductor's gestures.

    This is the simplest organizational technique for sound compositions. Other compositional ideas that use ECCO can be found in chapters 3 and 4.

4. Other ideas for families in ECCO are wooden sounds found in the kitchen; sounds from glass; sounds made from plastic; sounds made from things that are blue, red, green, and so on.

THE ELEMENTS OF MUSIC

Some terms have already been introduced that describe the qualities of music. In the following activities, a working description and an activity to illustrate the concept will be given for rhythm, tone/pitch, melody, harmony, timbre, texture, and musical controls. The brilliant composer and music philosopher from Canada, R. Murray Schafer, has done more to define our beliefs about music and its components than anyone else. We strongly recommend his book *Creative Music Education*. Schafer has the uncanny ability to define musical elements in new and unusual ways so as to crystallize their meaning.

Rhythm

Rhythm is direction. Rhythm exists in music when more than one sound is played horizontally. Rhythm has been called the heartbeat of music. "An adequate definition of rhythm comes close to defining music itself," says Roger Sessions, a contemporary American composer.[1] Rhythm consists of two separate entities: the pulse or beat, and the melodic rhythm.

Rhythm Play

Concepts: Experiencing rhythmic and melodic pulse.

Materials: None required.

Ages: 6 and up.

The following are simple, easy activities that use songs everyone knows.

1. Sing a familiar tune like "Row, row, row your boat." Clap according to the diagram below.

2. Now sing it again and clap according to the words as follows:

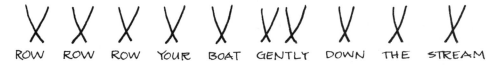

   The first time, students clap the pulse or beat of the music. The second time, they clap the rhythm of the melody.

3. To create an interesting rhythmic exercise, use the same song or a different one. Half of the class uses a body or found sound to perform the rhythmic beat or pulse of the music. The other half uses a different sound to perform the melodic beat.

4. With older students, divide into small groups and let each group choose a tune to perform. Have the rest of the class guess what the tune is.

Tone/Pitch

A tone is a sound of definite pitch and duration, whether created by an instrument, voice, machine, or nature. The *pitch* indicates the location of the tone in relation to another tone. Pitch is determined by the rate of vibrations—very slow vibrations create low pitches; very fast vibrations create high pitches. Many sound makers (including the human voice) can create a variety of pitches.

Ear Harps

Concepts: Exploring the properties of musical tones.

Materials: Rubber bands of varying thicknesses and sizes, jar lids, masking tape.

Ages: 7 and up.

Each student makes a small ear harp to experiment with tone and pitch.

1. Put a rubber band diametrically around a lid and secure it with tape to the lid's top. The bottom side is where the harp is plucked. The sound can be best heard if the harp is plucked close to the ear.

2. Encourage students to vary the pitch of their tone by stretching the rubber band. Have students add rubber bands of a different thickness to their harps, experimenting to create different tones and pitches.

Melody

A melody is like a tone going for a walk—a horizontal "line" across the music. A melody is what we remember about the music. Melodies can be pretty, ungainly, fluid, or angular. A melody can have one tone or many tones. It can have repeated tones or various tones. Each period of music history has its own definition of what a melody is. This activity explores the properties of a melody.

Melody Mix-Up

Concepts: Experiencing how melody works.

Materials: Long ribbon.

Ages: 6 and up.

Visualizing a melody helps students understand how music moves.

1. Take a long piece of ribbon and have two students hold the ribbon tight. As another student or teacher walks the length of the ribbon, have students sing the "pitch"

represented by the ribbon. Their pitch should not change because the ribbon is being held straight. If this straight ribbon were a real "walk" (melody), what kind would it be?

2. Now add more students to hold the line where they wish. It might look something like this:

The class is given the beginning tone and, following the teacher, "sings" the line, changing the tone as the ribbon changes direction. Is this a more interesting walk? What happens to the pitch?

3. Play around with this activity for a while. Students love it. It is an excellent way to begin a critical analysis. How could the melody be more pleasant or easier to sing? Should you add more contours? Less? A good melody does not have too many changes, nor is it too repetitious.

Harmony

Harmony is difficult to describe but easy to hear. Harmony is to music what perspective is to painting. It is the "verticalness" of music that occurs when more than one pitch is sounded simultaneously. It adds dimension and background to a piece of music. Harmony, like melody, has changed throughout musical history. Harmony can be consonant or dissonant. Harmony can only exist when there is more than one line of music, but both lines must be pitched, not just rhythmic. For example, if you sang "Row, row, row your boat" while you clapped the pulse, that would not be harmony even though there are two lines of music—the melody and the beat. With some help in listening, students as young as six can hear whether the harmony is consonant or dissonant.

Have You Heard the Harmony?

Concepts: Learning to hear consonant and dissonant harmonies.

Materials: Three glasses.

Ages: 8 and up.

1. Take three glasses and fill with different amounts of water. Each glass will give a different pitch when tapped on the outside along its rim. Find three that sound pleasing when struck simultaneously. This is consonant harmony. Experiment with the amounts of water and find three that sound harsh when the glasses are struck simultaneously. This is dissonant harmony. If students can make a sound by blowing into a bottle, then use three bottles filled with different amounts of water, instead of glasses.

Timbre

Timbre is the color of music. When we use our voice in speaking, we naturally use many timbres, from a whisper to a shout. Each instrument or sound maker has its own particular timbre. For instance, the clarinet has a dark, rich sound; the flute has a more whispery timbre.

Toying with Timbres

Concepts: Discovering different timbres in the voice.

Materials: None required.

Ages: 10 and up.

This is fun to do in small groups. Have each group perform for the class.

1. Give each group a sheet of paper with "Timbre is the tone color of the note" written at the top.

2. Have students explore all possibilities of saying this sentence with voice. Whispering, opening or closing the mouth, opening or closing just the lips or the teeth, and using the back or front of the throat will vary the voice. Volume of voice will also affect the timbre. Have each student say one word of the sentence, linking them together in order. Have students listen for different timbres.

3. For younger students, share the picture book *Five Live Bongos* by George Ella Lyon. This book contains a wide variety of found sounds, words, and colors that accurately describe the timbre of each sound.

Texture

Like a woven piece of cloth, the texture of a piece of music is determined by both its horizontal and vertical lines. Some music is thinly woven. Other music is quite dense. A musical composition's texture is often based on the types of instruments and the quantity used in the composition.

Weaving with Sounds

Concepts: Experiencing textures in music.

Materials: Sound sources—found sounds, body sounds, vocal sounds, or instrumental sounds; chalkboard or poster board; colored chalk or markers.

Ages: 10 and up.

1. Using colored chalk, draw illustrations on the chalkboard similar to the two figures below (or use poster board and markers).

2. Tell students to look at the two graphic illustrations. Which one has the clearer texture? Which one the thicker?

3. Use each of these illustrations as a musical score. Have students choose their own sounds, but the teacher should decide how many different sounds will be used. "Conduct" (trace the lines) as students perform. If the line squiggles, the sound should "squiggle"; if the line goes up, the sound should go up; and so on. More than one conductor might be needed for the more complicated figure above.

4. After students perform each picture, evaluate their performances. Which was easier to listen to? Why? Again, just as with melody and harmony, people in some periods of history preferred music that was dense, thick, and complex (e.g., nineteenth-century Brahms), and those in other times enjoyed clean, clear, distinct sounds (e.g., Renaissance Madrigal).

5. An elaboration of this activity, "Painting with Sounds," can be found in chapter 4. There are activities in chapters 1, 3, and 4 that use visual images for musical and storytelling activities, which is one of the most effective ways to understand the techniques of these art forms. Try one of these activities.

Musical Controls

Musical controls add interest to the musical elements. Volume (loudness) and tempo (speed) are two musical controls that can make melody, rhythm, timbre, texture, and harmony more interesting.

The Storm (A Concerto for Paper)

Concepts: Creating simple sound compositions.

Materials: Paper.

Ages: 7 and up.

From typing paper to various grades of cardboard, paper is a wonderful source for sound. Paper can be used as a found sound or as material for making instruments, such as the guiro (see "Guiro" in chapter 5).

1. In the classroom, have students pass a piece of paper as quietly as possible around the room. Discuss how the experience felt. How did students pass the paper? How did they handle the paper? Was it difficult to control the volume of the sound?

2. Now have the class pass the paper as loudly as possible. Discuss the contrast. Undoubtedly, students will pass the paper quickly, with little concern about the quality of the experience. The paper will probably be ripped to shreds. Discuss the difference between the two experiences. The first time, passing the paper softly, required more concentration, thought, and cooperation among all involved than the second experience. This process parallels the difference between making musical sounds and making noise.

3. Have each student create their own unique sound with a piece of paper. They can use something in addition to paper if they wish. Go around the room so everyone can hear the interesting sounds students create.

4. Tell a story with just paper sounds. A simple one is "The Storm." This story begins as does a storm, with all sounds quiet and mysterious (wind rustling leaves softly). As the storm builds, the sounds do, too (different paper sounds that are stronger and louder). At its strongest, the storm is very loud (thunder crashes, etc.). Gradually, the storm goes away and the sounds reverse themselves. One person can conduct the sounds, as per the environmental orchestra suggestions in this chapter (see the activity "The Environmental Orchestra"). The class can agree to all make specific sounds, or students can group into different stages of the storm, or they can decide what their individual sounds would best represent.

   When the composition has been performed, discuss whether it sounded like a storm they remember. What words describe the sounds of the storm? Try performing the musical piece again, but this time with the teacher saying the words that were suggested at appropriate moments during the performance.

5. For older students, a variation would be for small groups to determine a theme, discover various paper sounds to represent that theme, and improvise a sound story such as this one.

Repetition and Contrast

Most works of art are organized around the two basic elements of repetition and contrast. Repetition is the element that gives us comfort and familiarity, and contrast is the element of the unknown that makes something intriguing and exciting. In general, what most people consider a "good" work of art contains both elements. What is interesting is how the creator chooses to apply these structural elements. What repeats? What contrasts?

In the collaborative activities in this chapter there are exercises that stress this important structural and aesthetic element.

Say It Again

Concepts: Learning to hear repetition and contrast in music.

Materials: Pictures (animal and nature scenes work well); music selection: "Dance of the Toy Flutes" (Tchaikovsky), "Blue Rondo a la Turk" (Brubeck), or third movement of the "Pathétique" sonata (Beethoven).

Ages: 8 and up.

Repetition and contrast in music can be difficult to hear. The three pieces listed above have musical phrases that repeat often and so are easily distinguished from contrasting phrases.

1. Choose one picture to represent the repeated phrase. Play the selection, holding up the picture before the class each time the repeating phrase is heard.

2. Give each student a picture. Choose one student to hold the "repeating" picture. Play the selection again, having students hold up their pictures at the appropriate times (i.e., when the contrasting sections are heard, every student but the one designated to represent the repeating phrase will hold up their picture).

3. After students understand how repetition and contrast sound, they can create their own repeat/contrast/repeat piece with two contrasting sounds or patterns. For example, shaking sound / whistling / shaking sound / clapping / shaking sound / finger snapping. Divide students into sound groups and "conduct" a performance.

COLLABORATIVE ACTIVITIES

Relating Sounds to Words

Concepts: Exploring the relationship between words and musical sounds.

Materials: Chalkboard.

Ages: 8 and up.

Some sounds can be easily translated into verbal language; for instance, "click" for tongue click; "clap" for hand clap, and so on. Here are two activities that show relationships between words and sounds.

1. Have students think of vocal-body sounds and then invent words for them. The words can be as unusual as desired. For example, a cheek pop sound could be described with the word "ploop." List all the new words on the board. Have each student make their own sound. The class tries to figure out which word matches the sound.

2. Now make a list of particularly descriptive words like *ridiculous*, *persuasion*, *forbidden*, *exotic*, and *extraordinary*. Using the musical elements they have become familiar with, students say the words musically. For instance, they can use different pitches; repeat parts; elongate parts; slur the word; cut it up; say it fast, slow, loud, soft; and so on. The point is to make the word sound like its meaning. This is called "word painting" and has been used as a musical technique for centuries. Johann Sebastian Bach was a master at word painting. For example:

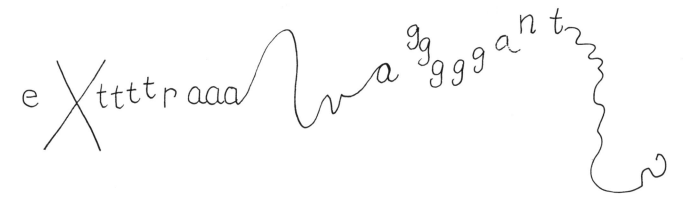

Describing Words Through Sounds

Concepts: Exploring the relationship between the meanings and sounds of words.

Materials: Sound sources—found sounds, body sounds, vocal sounds; chalkboard; paper; markers.

Ages: 10 and up.

1. Pair up students and give each pair a word to describe through any sound except saying the word itself. Encourage students to use found sounds, body sounds, and unusual vocal sounds. Try to avoid excessive body language. Try the following suggestions: fright, cold, love, anger, loneliness, disgust, jealousy, excitement, boredom, sympathy. These are all basic emotions that can be found in works of art or be responses to works of art. When emotions are present in a work of art, they are considered aesthetic elements that contribute to the value of the piece.

   Have students perform their sounds while the rest of the class tries to guess the emotion or reaction they are suggesting. Because you want the class to guess the word by the sound only, have the students who are creating the sounds stand behind a screen or have their backs to the class. Facial gestures often will give the word away.

2. Variation: Another way to describe words with sounds is to have each student draw, as originally as possible, their name on a large piece of paper. The more elaborate, the better. Each student then follows the shapes and curves to musically say their name. Put groups of students together to create their own musical compositions by arranging their musical names in patterns.

The Name Game

Concepts: Exploring musical elements.

Materials: Index cards of phrases (see below), blank index cards, basket.

Ages: 10 and up.

Here is another way to use words as a stimulus for exploring musical elements, particularly timbre, but also rhythm, melody, and pitch. Each student writes their name on an index card and puts it into a basket. On separate cards, provide phrases that indicate to each student how to say their name (see list below). Students draw a new name at random from the basket and take a phrase card. They each say their new name according to the directions. Go around the room, having students introduce themselves to each other with the new names. Then each student finds who had their real name and how they said it. The following are some suggestions:

as loudly as possible	as softly as possible
with no consonants	with no vowels
backward	as a rap
emphasizing vowels	from very high to very low
with mouth wide open	through the teeth
like a tennis game	as fast as possible
like a Slinky™	with a floating quality
with an echo	as angrily as possible
as neutrally as possible	as funny as possible
as slowly as possible	like a fish
emphasizing consonants	like the wind
like you're really far away	like a machine
from very low to very high	like an explosion
like you've just seen a ghost	like you're sucking a lemon

The above exercise introduces to students a wide variety of ways that musical elements and other effects can be incorporated into words to create interesting, simple, musical ideas. These musical elements and controls are also vital tools for a storyteller's craft.

ECCO Meets Jack—A Sound Story

Concepts: Orchestrating a story.

Materials: Index cards, found sounds (see the activity "The Environmental Orchestra" in this chapter).

Ages: 10 and up.

Preparation: Write the following phrases on index cards, one phrase per card: clouds floating, sparks flying, walking, tossing and dropping a penny, donkey braying, cat hissing and spitting, pouring milk, cheese melting, getting married, dragging ham, smiling and laughing.

1. Divide students into eleven groups and give each group one phrase card. Have students discover found sounds that best describe their phrase. Next, list the four families of ECCO (the Environmentally Correct Chamber Orchestra): nature sounds, human sounds, man-made sounds, and animal sounds. Have students determine which family their sounds belong to. Have student groups come together into these four large families for a performance. Choose a conductor who will assist the "musicians" in their entrances. That person should have the order of phrases (in italics) found in the story below. The teacher should read or tell the story of "Lazy Jack" (below) while students make their sounds when they are mentioned in the story, following the conductor's lead.

2. When students create their sounds, encourage them not to use words like "meow" but nonverbal sounds—vocal, body, or found. For example, "getting married" might be represented by closing a purse zipper, thus effectively combining a sound with a visual representation of union.

Lazy Jack

Retold by Barbara M. Britsch

Once there was a boy named Jack who lived with his mother in a small house outside of town. They were very poor. The only money they had came from the wool of their one sheep, which the mother sold in town.

Now, Jack was very lazy. All winter he sat in front of the fire and watched the *sparks fly* up the chimney. In the summer, he lay in the fields watching the *clouds floating* overhead. So, he was called Lazy Jack.

As Jack grew and got taller, he ate more and more. One day his mother said, "Jack, I can't buy or grow enough food to feed you. You are going to have to get a job and earn some money."

Jack, who had a good heart, said, "I know, Mother. Tomorrow I'll go to town and find a job." And so he did. He *walked* into the town, to the market square, where, on the notice board, he saw a sign that said, "Wanted— Farmer's Helper." Jack took that sign and *walked* through the town into the country.

Jack worked all day for that farmer, and, for a lazy boy, he worked hard. He mended fences, milked the cows, and cleaned out the stables. At the end of the day, the farmer paid him with a large, shiny silver penny.

Now, that may not seem like much money today, but in those days, that penny was good money, especially for a boy like Jack who had never had a penny in his pocket.

Jack took that penny and started *walking* home, *tossing* the penny in the air and catching it, *tossing* and catching, *tossing* and catching, watching it glint in the sun. To get home, Jack had to cross a swiftly running stream. Just in the middle of the bridge, when he *tossed* the penny—he missed! The penny *dropped* in the water and was swept away, and Jack had to *walk* all the way home and tell his mother he had lost his day's pay.

"Oh, Jack," cried his mother. "How could you be so silly? You should have put the penny into your pocket."

"I'm sorry, mother," said Jack. "I'll remember—pocket."

The next day Jack went to work for a dairyman, and again he worked hard. At the end of the day, the dairyman paid him with a pitcher of fresh milk. Jack remembered what his mother had said. He opened up his pocket and *poured* in all the milk. Well, he had not taken two steps before all the milk was gone, and once again Jack had to *walk* home and tell his mother that his day's pay was lost.

"Ja-a-ack," said his mother. "What shall I do with you? You should have carried the pitcher on your head!"

"Oh," said Jack. "On my head. Right. I'll remember."

The next day Jack worked for another farmer. He cleaned out a lot of stables that day, and when he was through, the farmer paid Jack with a large cream cheese, round and soft. It smelled delicious. Jack remembered what his mother had told him and carried that cheese home on his head. But it was a long *walk*, and the sun was shining down. The cheese began to *melt*. It ran down through Jack's hair, all over his clothes, and by the time Jack got home, he was a mess, and there was no cheese left.

"Jack!" cried his mother. "What a foolish boy you are! You should have wrapped the cheese in cool green leaves and carried it in your hands."

"I'm sorry," said Jack. "Cool green leaves. Hands. Right. I'll remember."

The next day, Jack went to work for a baker in the town. He liked working in the bakery. He rolled out the dough for cinnamon rolls and sold chocolate chip cookies, and once, when no one was looking, he ate one. Now, this baker was not the nicest man. He thought, "I'll pay this boy with that mean, scrawny cat that's always hanging around here." And that is just what he did. Jack remembered what his mother had said. He picked some fresh green leaves and tried to wrap them around the cat. But the cat would not stand for that. It *hissed and spat* and clawed, jumped out of Jack's hands, and ran away. So once more, Jack had to *walk* home to tell his mother he had no pay.

"What were you thinking?" said his mother. "You should have tied a string around its neck and led it home."

"I am sorry, mother," said Jack. "I'll remember. String."

The next day, Jack worked for a butcher, cutting up meat all day. At the end of the day, the butcher gave him, for pay, a whole ham. Oh, it looked tasty! Jack, remembering what his mother had told him, tied a string around the ham and *dragged* it through the dirt as he walked home. Of course, the ham was ruined.

"Jack!" cried his mother. "How stupid can you be? You should have carried it home on your shoulder."

The next day, Jack worked for a man who raised and sold horses and mules and donkeys. He worked so hard that at the end of the day the man paid Jack with what was probably his best pay so far—a real live donkey! Not a full-grown donkey, a young one, but still a live animal. Jack, remembering what his mother had said, with a lot of trouble, got his shoulder under the donkey, and pushed and pulled until he had that donkey on his back. The donkey, of course, was *braying* and kicking. Jack set off *walking* home, and I want to tell you, he took a short cut.

He passed by the house of a rich merchant. This merchant had a daughter who was beautiful, clever, wise, and kind—like a perfect person. But there was one thing she had never done in her whole life. She had never *laughed* or even *smiled*. Her father was so worried about this that he said that any man who could make her *laugh* or even *smile* could have her for his wife. You see, in those days, fathers could give away their daughters. I'm glad we don't do that anymore.

Now, picture this. Here comes Jack *walking* down the street, carrying the donkey—which was kicking and *braying*. The girl looked out the window. This was the silliest thing she had ever seen, and before she knew what was happening, the corners of her mouth turned up—she *smiled*! Then a little *laugh* came out—quite rusty at first, but soon she was *laughing and laughing*! Her father was delighted. He ran out in the street and said to Jack, "Put down that donkey and come with me." He told Jack the story of his daughter.

Well, Jack and the girl were happy to be *married*. Jack's mother came to live with them, and they did not have to worry about money any more. And Jack—well, he could be as lazy as he wanted.

NOTES

1. Joseph Machlis, *The Enjoyment of Music* (New York: W. W. Norton, 1977), 19.

REFERENCES

Recordings

Beethoven, Ludwig van. *Sonata no. 8 in C, op. 13, "Pathétique."* Arrau. Philips 420153-2 PH (CD).

Brubeck, Dave. *Blue Rondo a la Turk.* Concord Records CDJ 00204 (CD).

Tchaikovsky, Piotr Ilyich. "Dance of the Toy Flutes," from *The Nutcracker Suite, op. 71A.* Suisse Romande. Ansermet. London 417097-4LT (cassette).

———. "Dance of the Toy Flutes," from *The Nutcracker Suite, op. 71A.* New York Philharmonic Orchestra. CBS MYK-37238 (CD); MYT-37238 (cassette).

Books

Ahlberg, Janet, and Allen Ahlberg. *The Jolly Postman: Or Other People's Letters.* New York: Little, Brown, 1985.

Barrett, Judi. *Cloudy with a Chance of Meatballs.* Illustrated by Ron Barrett. New York: Atheneum, 1978.

Bunting, Eve. *The Man Who Could Call Down Owls.* Illustrated by Charles Mikolaycak. New York: Macmillan, 1984.

Domanska, Janina. *The Turnip.* New York: Macmillan, 1969.

Grahame, Kenneth. *The Wind in the Willows.* New York: Scribner's, 1908.

Hutchins, Pat. *Rosie's Walk.* New York: Macmillan, 1968.

Irving, Washington. *The Legend of Sleepy Hollow.* Illustrated by Robert Van Nutt. Saxonville, Mass.: Picture Book Studio, 1989.

Latimer, Jim. *When Moose Was Young.* New York: Scribner's, 1990.

Locker, Thomas. *The Land of Gray Wolf.* New York: Dial, 1991.

Lyon, George Ella. *Five Live Bongos.* New York; Scholastic, 1994.

Martin, Rafe. *The Rough-Face Girl.* Illustrated by David Shannon. New York: G. P. Putnam's Sons, 1992.

McDermott, Gerald. *The Stonecutter.* New York: Viking Press, 1975.

Oughton, Jerrie. *How the Stars Fell into the Sky: A Navajo Legend.* Illustrated by Lisa Desimini. Boston: Houghton Mifflin, 1992.

Roberts, Bethany. *Waiting-for-Papa Stories.* Illustrated by Sarah Stapler. New York: Harper & Row, 1990.

———. *Waiting-for-Spring Stories.* Illustrated by William Joyce. New York: Harper & Row, 1984.

Rockwell, Anne *The Three Bears & 15 Other Stories.* New York: Thomas Y. Crowell, 1975.

Schafer, R. Murray. *Creative Music Education.* New York: Schirmer Books, 1976.

Stewig, John. *The Fisherman and His Wife.* Illustrated by Margot Tomes. New York: Holiday House, 1988.

Putting It All Together
Organization and Structure

All works of art, no matter how they appear at first glance, have some form of organization. In this chapter, we will explore how the elements of a story or piece of music are organized to create a work of art. As the Chinese proverb goes, "Tell me, I'll forget. Show me, I may remember. Involve me, I'll understand." This chapter allows students to actively engage in the organizational processes of stories and music. Their understanding of a work of art will be nurtured in the doing.

By considering the structural elements of a story or a piece of music, this chapter is, in effect, an extension of chapter 2, which looked closely at those elements individually. Here, the emphasis is on experimenting with parts to create a whole, on manipulating elements to create effective patterns and designs, thus building on the basic aesthetic principles in a work of art.

Stories and music make use of similar compositional designs, such as the repeated phrase, but each art form has its own unique organizational structure. As students work through these exercises, similarities in structure and design will become evident. The collaborative activities will bring together some structures and patterns evident in both art forms.

THE STRUCTURE OF STORIES

Although the enduring impact of a story is felt in one's generalized response to it (as pointed out in chapter 1), we can understand stories better and learn to construct our own tales as works of art by looking more closely at how literary elements, together, make up a story's substance. "Together" is the operative word. Plot events, characters, setting, point of view, and themes can be investigated individually as in chapter 2, but their interdependence creates an aesthetic whole.

When we ask students, "What was this story about?" they will inevitably recount the *plot*—what happened. Similarly, adults tend to focus on the events of a book or film. In doing so, both children and adults also speak of the *characters* involved: (for E. B. White's *Charlotte's Web*)"Its about how Charlotte—she's a spider—saved Wilbur the pig, and they became friends." We all respond to characters' behavior in a story, whether or not we like them, their appearance, their growth or lack of it, and their interaction with other characters.

It seems obvious to say that events and characters in a story always function in particular *settings*. Students, however, may not recognize that our understanding of characters' natures changes as their behavior, speech, and reactions change in response not only to what is happening but to where they are. The setting thus provides a context that likely will illuminate character's essential qualities.

Imagine how different our response would be to *Charlottes Web* if Templeton, the rat, had told the story. Experimenting with an alternate *point of view* is a familiar and worthwhile literary activity in classrooms, but an activity that will be enhanced by helping students see that changing the point of view is more than another character narrating the story. Not only is the angle of vision different, so is the *tone*.

Templeton's version of the Wilbur saga would be cynical and pessimistic, and his *language* acerbic. In addition, his view would be from the bottom of the pigsty, a narrow upward view, in contrast to the book's constantly shifting point of view: from omniscient to Wilbur to Charlotte to Fern to the various barnyard animals to Templeton, and so on, thus providing the widest view of Wilbur's world and a delightful range of language.

Just as music listeners can recognize organizational patterns in musical compositions or improvisations, so story listeners can identify story patterns. Just as composers can play with rhythm, melody, and timbre, so story creators can experiment with combinations of plot events, characters, settings, points of view, tone, and language. The storytelling activities in this chapter will provide opportunities for students and teacher, together, to explore these crucial relationships to discover how stories work.

The following activities are divided into two age-appropriate parts. "Exploring Story Patterns" encourages younger students (ages 5-7) to become actively involved in the overall design of several familiar story patterns, thus enhancing their recognition of story composition. Notice that the format of this section differs somewhat from that in chapters 1 and 2, with more variations offered for each activity. "Linking Up the Parts," the second section, contains story composition activities more appropriate for older students (ages 8-12).

Exploring Story Patterns

Among the most enduring and favorite tales for younger children are those with a predictable pattern, or formula. *The Little Red Hen* (Galdone), *The Gingerbread Man*, and *The Old Woman and Her Pig* (Rockwell) are examples of stories with easily remembered patterns that heighten anticipation of the familiar. Activities in this section are aimed at kindergarten and primary students, who readily respond with delight to such stories. Stories with sequential and cumulative patterns are the perfect introduction for this age group to how stories work.

As defined here, a sequential story has a series of events in which a basic pattern is repeated, but with a variation in each event. A familiar example is *The Three Bears* (Stewig), in which the pattern of use and destruction is repeated for each event (bowls of porridge, chairs, beds), as is the pattern of the bears' response to the parallel sequence of objects upon their return. In *The Fisherman and His Wife* (Stewig), the pattern of "wish, ritual verse, wish granted" elevates the wife until her greed breaks the pattern.

Cumulative stories also make use of repetition, but here the pattern is one of addition. Each previous event is repeated by the storyteller (with eager participation by the audience) as a new one is added. Familiar examples are *The Gingerbread Man, Henny Penny* (Rockwell), and *The Old Woman and Her Pig* (Rockwell). Some of these tales, such as the last two, also "unwind" the pattern by repeating the events backward in some fashion close to the end of the story.

A third pattern, similar to one found in musical composition, is "call and response," or "question and answer," as in *Happy Birthday, Moon* (Asch). Here, Bear's questions to the moon are echoed off the mountain, convincing Bear that he is indeed talking to the moon. *The Shepherd Boy*, found in *The Old Woman and Her Pig and 10 Other Stories* (Rockwell), is a short story consisting almost entirely of questions and answers between the shepherd boy and the king.

One of the most common patterns in folklore is that of repeating magical words, phrases, and verses, which illustrates the ancient power of the sound of language to make things happen. Repeated language is also found in contemporary literary stories, such as *Millions of Cats* (Gag) and *Where the Wild Things Are* (Sendak).

Pop-Ups

Concepts: Providing students with a verbal, auditory, physical, and visual experience of a cumulative story. Enhancing sorting skills.

Materials: Individual paddles (see below); "The Gingerbread Man," in *The Three Bears & 15 Other Stories* (Rockwell).

Ages: 5-7.

For this activity, each student (except those portraying the gingerbread man and the fox) should have a paddle cut from tagboard or foam core with an image of one of the story characters glued on. The images can be drawn by students or provided by teachers; they may consist of just a picture or a picture with the appropriate word. If using tagboard, reinforce the handles to hold up under repeated and enthusiastic use. The six characters should be duplicated so that there is a group of old men, old women, cows, horses, farmers, and children. Tell the story to the class before this activity, perhaps several times. Other sequential and cumulative stories are in the references at the end of this chapter.

1. Divide students into six groups according to the above characters. Arrange groups throughout the room, in the order they appear in the story, perhaps seated at the tables frequently found in kindergarten and primary rooms, or gathered together in the "storytelling ring." Select a gingerbread man and a fox.

2. Rehearse the characters' cues. For example, when the words "little old man" are said, that is the cue for the paddles showing the old man to "pop up." Otherwise they are facedown. Similarly for each set of characters.

3. The teacher, as storyteller and guide, travels with the gingerbread man through the landscape of the story while telling it. The telling should have a fairly leisurely pace so that cues are easily heard. The class can join in on the refrain, "I have run away from . . . ," or each group of characters may announce its name. Be inventive with the possibilities. The gingerbread man may say, "You can't catch me! I'm the Gingerbread Man!" Paddles should stay up throughout the repeated refrain, then be lowered as the adventure continues.

4. The fox is waiting at the last station of the story, the river, to "carry" the gingerbread man across. Ask the gingerbread man and the fox to do a stylized "freeze" at the end rather than trying to show the fox eating the gingerbread man.

5. Variation: As the point here is to focus students' attention on repeated patterns through seeing, listening, speaking, and movement, this activity can assume many forms. The emphasis is not so much on the sites or stations of the story as on the cumulative effect of the *characters'* verbal responses to the gingerbread man. If paddles seem too distracting, students may use their hands, perhaps with different colored ribbons tied around the wrist. Each group might wish to have its own symbol or representation of its character placed on the table or floor. Appropriate sounds might be added for each character: for example, a particular laugh ("hee, hee") for the little old man, or the obvious animal sounds for the cow and horse. If you plan to use the whole room, map the gingerbread man's journey: with a butcher paper trail on the floor, with yarn or ribbon, or with anything appropriate. Add an interesting river location.

6. Variation: The story *Too Much Noise*, by Ann McGovern, displays the "unwinding" pattern of cumulative stories. As the action takes place in Peter's house and that of the wise man, the setup requires only two primary locations, plus a "stockade" where Peter can pick up each animal to add to his increasingly crowded house. Also required are props to represent a bed, a floor, wind, leaves, and a tea kettle. For all of these, as well as the animals, student-produced sounds are a natural addition. Simple headbands are another possibility for character identification. Again, it is the characters who provide the cumulative effect. This will be a busier and noisier story to play out than "The

Gingerbread Man," as Peter makes the journey from home to wise man to stockade to home many times, with the noise increasing each time. That very structure, however, will demonstrate dramatically the welcome silence he eventually finds.

7. Variation: You might wish to add simple concepts of addition and subtraction for beginning math by assigning a sequence of numbers (1, 2, 3, etc.), one to each group, in some fashion (e.g., on the paddles).

One Thing After Another

Concepts: Providing students with a verbal, auditory, physical, and visual experience of a sequential story.

Materials: "The Three Little Pigs," in *The Three Bears & 15 Other Stories* (Rockwell); other sequential stories (see below); tagboard; cardboard paper-towel tubes; three Hula Hoop® spinning toys.

Ages: 6-7.

In this activity involving sequential stories, the emphasis is on individual episodes at various locations, to convey the idea that some things change and some remain the same. This is obviously true of cumulative stories as well, but sequential stories do not have the verbal *additions and subtractions*. They only have *repeated* language and actions. Tell the story several times to the class before this activity. There are additional sequential stories listed at the end of this chapter.

1. Place the hoops at three clearly separate sites in a cleared space in the classroom, thus defining each site of the story while allowing the action to proceed smoothly.

2. Assign character roles to students: the mother pig; the three little pigs; three men with straw, sticks, and bricks; and the wolf. Assign two or three students to each hoop to represent the house walls. Remaining students become the audience. Have students sit next to their hoops; then, as each house is built by the appropriate pig, have the "house wall" students stand and show—with hands, arms, body, and so on—how their particular house looks: straw sticks out and looks prickly; sticks look twiggy, like small branches; brick is obviously so substantial that it cannot be moved. As the wolf blows down the first two houses, have those "house wall" students collapse onto the floor next to their hoops. So students will not bump into one another, have them perform their movements in slow motion.

3. As in the activity "Pop-ups," the narrator leads the characters through the action of the story, with all students chiming in on the repeated phrases (e.g., "I'll huff and I'll puff . . ."). Repeat steps 2 and 3 with the audience half of the class.

4. For the students waiting their turn, emphasize the importance of the audience. There would be no story without an audience to respond, participate, watch, and listen. This is a cooperative experience, as important for the listeners as it is for the participants

and teller. The story comes alive, not only in the played-out action but in the mind's eye of each listener. Give the audience specific things to notice. Ask, "How will these students make this house look like straw? Or twigs? Or brick?" or, "Will the wolf move in a way that tells you what he's thinking?" Questions such as these will help students in the audience focus more closely on characters' actions, which will encourage better performances during their turn.

5. Variation: The sequential pattern of "The Three Billy Goats Gruff," in *The Three Bears & 15 Other Stories*, differs from that of "The Three Little Pigs" in that the primary action takes place in one location, the bridge. As the language in this story is almost entirely repetitive, focus on the *difference* of each event by enhancing the character of each goat. The youngest may be timid (or perhaps brash), with a short, curly, white coat and no horns. The middle goat is "middlin' " in every way—light brown coat and medium ideas. The big goat is, of course, commanding, with large, curved horns and a heavy, shaggy coat. Each moves differently, sounds different on the bridge, and so on. Ask the class for suggestions for the goats and for the troll, who may be as horrible as they wish. Note that the troll does not die; he disappears. To accommodate more students, place some into two lines for the bridge. Several students can compose each goat and the troll, again with an appropriate visual image. Dramatize the story twice, as above. Each time, ask the audience to watch characters' movements closely—"How do students *show* their characters through action?"

6. Variation for ages 4-5: Tell the story with students seated in a group and provided with simple tagboard shapes of different sizes and colors representing the three billy goats (small, medium, and large) and the troll. The goats should be represented by circles of respective size; the darker the color, the larger the goat. The troll should be represented by an abstract shape, perhaps with points. Glue a paper-towel tube to the back of each circle so that characters can trit-trot across the bridge or rise dramatically from the river. As students manipulate their shapes in response to characters' roles, the story should take on a rhythm that will emphasize its structure. Simple, rhythm instrument sounds can be added for each character, so that the story experience becomes a combination of visual, musical, and linguistic elements.

Clues, More Clues

Concepts: Enhancing a sense of plot sequence. Developing simple mapping
        skills. Developing spatial concepts.

Materials: *The Secret Birthday Message* (Carle), writing and art materials (see
        below).

Ages: 6-8.

Constructing their own codes and secrets, as demonstrated in Carle's engaging book, will capture both eager and reluctant readers. The use of graphic shapes, rather than letters or numbers, is appropriate for primary age students as they invent a trail for their character to follow. The trail itself becomes a story sequence—one mini-event after another—an effective and simple story-mapping device. Inventing the trail also develops spatial concepts of "over, under, around, through," and so on.

1. Read *The Secret Birthday Message* to the class, showing the clue shapes and predicting what will come next.

2. As a class, invent a new trail for Tim or your own character to follow. It might be another birthday present to find, a secret from a friend or parent, or perhaps something a teacher has hidden for a class. Sketch the trail on the board, then decide on the graphic shapes as clues for each site. Your trail might be under the ocean or in the sky, rolling and jumping from planet to cloud to star to moon. Classrooms offer possibilities for a trail.

3. For your story, construct either a class book, perhaps a "big book," individual books, or books by small groups. With each student or group contributing a page, keep a generous left-hand margin for punching or stapling. See chapter 6 for simple bookbinding directions.

4. The pages in Carle's book have shaped edges and cutouts. See chapter 6, "Japanese Folding Book," for further suggestions on using this technique. The pages may simply be cut and drawn with markers, crayons, or colored pencils, and the text appropriately placed; or you may wish to experiment with collage, pasting on clue shapes and objects using a variety of art papers.

5. Discuss with the class that the sequence of events is critical in this treasure hunt. Just as in other stories, one event cannot happen until something else takes place. As your class reads and hears other stories throughout the year, occasionally approach them as if they were a "treasure hunt," looking for "clues" that help predict what might come next.

Linking the Parts

Imagine This

Concepts: Exploring story composition. Enhancing visual imagery.

Materials: Writing and drawing supplies.

Ages: 8-10.

The following sequence of activities should be spread over several days, perhaps weeks. Give students plenty of time to write their stories.

1. Have students close their eyes and mentally picture the following description as the teacher reads it (or the teacher can invent another description following a pattern of "journey, arrival, discovery").

Imagine you are in a rowboat on a river with your best friend. The two of you share the rowing. As your friend rows, you feel the warm sun on your face; you see how the water sparkles; willow trees lean over the riverbank. In the distance, you see an island. Your friend rows toward it. At first, you see only dark trees, but as you come closer, you see bushes, plants, and flowers. The boat glides onto a sandy beach. You and your friend get out, anchor the boat, and walk across the beach. The sand is warm and soft under your feet. You see a path through the trees. As you start to walk up this path, you hear birds sing, but not like any birds you've ever heard. You notice the leaves on the trees—

2. Stop at any appropriate moment and quietly ask students to imagine, for example, what the birds sound like and what the leaves might look like. Students should not give oral responses but should see it in their mind's eye. Ask students to imagine the whole scene: the path beneath their feet (sandy? mossy? covered with leaves?), the trees (height, colors, types), flowers, bushes, plants, birds (size, colors, songs).

3. At this point, students may draw their scene to use as a visual prompt for a story (see below), or they may write a one-paragraph description of this scene.

4. Brainstorm with the class some possibilities for the continuation of individual stories, stressing that each story will be different, with no more than three events. This is the time to review story structure (beginning, middle, and end); that events relate to each other; that characters interact; and so forth. There are endless possible plots: An animal or other character in the woods needs help. Students discover a tree with a door in the trunk—what is inside? Students discover a forest pool with steps that lead underwater—what is there? Encourage students to stay true to their vision, that is, would they be likely to find Roadrunner or Dr. Mario in this setting?

5. Now have students write out their stories in detail. You may encourage students to invent alternate beginnings. The setting may not be an island, but a mysterious country road or a path in a park they know.

6. Compare two or more students' stories that have the same or similar characters and plot events, stressing the differences as individual visions.

7. Gather these stories into a class book, asking students to submit illustrations.

In Shape

Concepts: Enhancing visual perception and divergent thinking. Practicing story composition.

Materials: One or more of the following: art posters, calendar pictures, slides of fine art paintings, picture-book illustrations; drawing materials.

Ages: 9-12.

This activity begins with one art form and ends with another: from visual art to literature, encouraging divergent thinking.

1. Select one picture—either abstract, such as a painting by Miró, or representational, perhaps an illustration from a picture book. If you choose the latter, use one unfamiliar to the class to encourage close looking.

2. Display the picture, asking, "What do you see?" Accept all answers. For an abstract painting, responses may be quite different from your expectations. This step helps students to focus closely on the work, encouraging them to respond to and interpret lines, shapes, spaces, and colors.

3. Next, define several specific shapes in the picture by outlining them with a pointer. In a representational picture, these may be the sweep of a cloak, the shape of a hat brim, or negative space (e.g., the sky as seen through tree branches). Avoid easily recognizable shapes such as a house, shoe, or chair. Shapes should be as abstract as possible. Draw two or three of these shapes on chalkboard, then ask students to find other shapes in other pictures displayed or use one of your models. Each student finds a shape and draws its outline on drawing paper.

4. Each student's outline now becomes the basis for an imaginary creature. Students add onto the shape as desired. The shape may be seen as an eye, a toe, an antenna, and so on. Give the class time to explore possibilities. Model this step for them.

5. Once creatures are invented, ask students to write the answers to three questions on the same paper: Where does this creature live? What does it eat? What is its name?

6. These drawings are now the basis for original stories. In two's, students begin their stories by imagining a meeting between their two creatures. Where do they meet? What is the weather? How are they feeling? Perhaps they are on the way to a convention of monsters, called to consider a serious (or frivolous) question of concern to the monster population. Perhaps they are lost. Perhaps one creature has an object that the other

desires. Brainstorm possibilities with students before they begin their stories. Starting stories with a self-created prompt stimulates students' imaginations, and the structured approach gives the teacher the opportunity to guide use of literary elements.

7. Stories are outlined, written, or audiotaped. The results lend themselves well to creative drama and preservation in illustrated handmade books (see chapter 6).

First Lines

Concepts: Enhancing understanding of a story based on previous story "knowledge." Practicing story composition.

Materials: First lines from folktales (see samples below) written on cutout shapes such as feet (stories are journeys) or books (where we find stories); pictorial stimuli for stories with interesting, surprising, or mysterious depictions of people, places, or objects (art posters, calendar pictures, magazine pictures, etc.); writing materials.

Ages: 10-12.

This activity for older students focuses on the serious study of folklore. It is an activity of discovery and composition akin to musical improvisation. It works best at the end of a folklore unit in which students have heard and read many folktales and have discussed repeated patterns and motifs in these stories, perhaps similar tales from different cultures.

Some sample first lines are as follows:

"Once there was an old king who had three sons."

"Many years ago, the Emperor's palace was the most splendid in the world."

"In old Japan, in the far-off days, when dragons roamed the land . . ."

"There was a man who was not kind to animals."

"When the pulse of the first day carried it to the rim of night . . ."

"There was a poor widow before now and she had three daughters."

"Long, long ago when all the animals could talk, and even the birds and fishes could understand . . ."

"There was once a very rich gentleman with three daughters, and he thought he'd see how fond they were of him."

1. Display the cutout shapes with first lines in any convenient way: chalkboard, bulletin board, poster board, or on the floor. Read a few lines to the class, explaining that they lead us into the story.

2. Using two or three pictures, suggest possible first lines for a story about each picture. Ask class to do the same for other pictures, focusing on what they see. See the previous activity, "In Shape," for the complete procedure of interpreting what is seen.

3. Students select or are given a picture each and invent a possible first line to lead into the picture's story. The story, and thus its first line, will be in the folklore genre.

4. Next, as a group, look at the shapes with first lines again, asking the class to predict generally what the story may be about: setting, characters, one or two events. For example, the line "Once there was an old king who had three sons" suggests, based on our experience of folklore, that the setting is a castle, that the king sends his sons on a quest, that the youngest will succeed and inherit the kingdom. "There was a poor widow before now and she had three daughters" implies a cottage and the need to provide for her daughters. "Dragons" suggests adventure and danger in a wild outdoor setting. "When the pulse of the first day" implies a creation tale. Delaying this step until *after* students have written their own first lines allows them to discover how they used existing knowledge in composing their lines.

5. Ask several students to share their first lines with their pictures and to predict what their story might include. The discussion should be open to possibilities—this is improvisation. At the same time, first lines suggest probabilities. Discuss with students how their first lines show their existing knowledge of folktales.

6. Students compose their stories, in writing or on audiotape. Stories may be illustrated and recorded in handmade books (see chapter 6).

THE STRUCTURE OF MUSIC

Why do people make music? A possible answer suggested by Yehudi Menuhin, a musical master of this century, is that music's aesthetic value lies in its organization.[1] Making music is an intentional act. By exerting control over the artistic elements, human beings can make sense out of the world at large. Thus, a musical composition and, by extension, any created work of art, represent a microcosm of the universe. All the various symbolic methods we use to investigate the nature of the world and ourselves are found in music.

This rather esoteric, thought-provoking idea can be understood in much simpler terms. There is a basic need for organization in life, and each person finds their own solution to this need. In music, this need for organization is expressed in *composition*. Additionally, the concept of *choice* is a vital element in music composition.

In the introduction of this book, the basic role of the composer was outlined. This portion of chapter 3 is divided into two sections: improvisation and composition. Activities, experiences, and guided listening are offered as ways to involve students in the process of music. Compositional activities that use rhythm, melody, timbre, form, and musical controls are suggested. Any of the sounds discovered in earlier chapters can be used, depending on availability. These activities range from extremely simple, improvisatory activities to full-length, formal pieces. Traditional notation is optional in most cases; in fact, creating notation that reflects what the sounds are doing is a challenging and enjoyable part of the compositional process, especially for older students.

Improvisation

Improvisation can be defined as the simultaneous conception, creation, practice, and performance of a piece of music. Music educator Patricia Shehan Campbell has defined improvisation as "the spontaneous generation of melody and rhythm without specific preparation or premeditation. . . . [I]t is the musical response to an unpredictable impulse or feeling. . . . [I]t is the intricate balance of performance and composition, all at once."[2] When we think of improvisation, we might conjure up images of dimly lit, smoke-filled bars with spaced-out saxophone players wearing dark glasses and berets, à la the 1960s. Yes, improvisation plays a vital role in jazz and indeed helps define that musical form. Nonetheless, improvisation has been an intrinsic part of Western music since the early beginnings in Greek times and for many centuries after, when music was sparsely notated, if at all. During the Baroque period in Europe (see the section "Music History" in chapter 4), all musicians were required to develop improvisational skills, and it is a well-known fact that the great composers all improvised. In cultures where folk music dominates the musical scene, improvisation is a key element in music making.

In the classroom, improvisational activities can be used when you have some time to fill. These activities can introduce a more complicated music and story project, or they can be used to "test" something just learned—a new instrument or sound, a poem, or a concept. In addition, improvisational activities can be used to explore composition.

Before beginning any improvisational musical activities, reflect with students on how improvisation is a part of everyday life. Ask them questions such as the following: Did you ever plan to cook something and find you did not have a certain ingredient? Did you ever discover that a favorite television show was preempted by a special report? Have you ever gone to a restaurant and discovered they were out of a favorite dish? In each of these situations, you were faced with a spontaneous decision, in the same way a musical improviser confronts a certain given set of circumstances.

Even in something as "free" as an improvised activity, however, a given set of circumstances must be stated. A goal or objective to the activity must be understood, and guidelines to follow to achieve that goal need to be stated. As all teachers know, students respond and learn more effectively when given guidelines and parameters.

Unfortunately, too many professional musicians and music teachers have gone through the educational system that promotes "eye" music, that is, relying on the written page of music. Improvisational music is "ear" music, more like that of folk cultures around the world, in which the performers rely on what they hear, not what they read. Though choice is a critical element in both composition and improvisation, the improviser has more choices than the player who performs notated music. The improviser has choices regarding notes, tempo, dynamics, accents, rhythms, and sound sources—sometimes all these choices simultaneously.

Name That Tune

Concepts: Providing starting points for simple improvisation exercises.

Materials: None required.

Ages: 6 and up.

Simple activities to do whenever you wish!

1. Choose a familiar song. Sing it to a different tune.

2. Choose a familiar song. Sing it to a different tempo.

3. Choose a familiar song. Change the accents of the words.

Can You Beat That?

Concepts: Creating rhythmic patterns based on a steady, underlying beat.

Materials: Music selection from *Rhythmically Moving* (Gemini) or *Hooked on Classics* recordings.

Ages: 8 and up.

Any of the *Rhythmically Moving* or *Hooked on Classics* recordings are ideal for this particular activity (see references at the end of this chapter for these and other recordings).

1. Taking Turns: Use one of the suggested musical recordings with a strong, steady beat. With students in a circle, each student takes a turn to individually improvise an eight-beat percussion pattern, keeping with the rhythmic pulse; the rest of the class watches.

2. Call and Response: Going around the circle again, each student improvises an eight-beat pattern to the music; the rest of the class imitates the pattern.

3. Rondo: Determine an eight-beat pattern and have the class learn it. Alternate that pattern with individual eight-beat improvisations. (This is similar to the activity "Say It Again," in chapter 2.)

Jump to the Music

Concepts: Exploring patterns of sound and silence.

Materials: Four Hula Hoop® spinning toys, sound source for each student (body, found sounds, simple instruments).

Ages: 8 and up.

This is a simple and effective way to visualize the organization of sound patterns.

1. One person is appointed as conductor. The class sits in a circle with their sound sources, and the conductor stands in the middle in the hula hoop. The conductor creates patterns of sound and silence by body movements in and out of the hoop. The class responds to the conductor's movements by making sounds. By varying the energy level of the movements, the conductor can suggest how the sound should be created. For instance, a light tap of the toe in the hoop would suggest a soft, light sound; a huge jump with both feet in would call for a loud, heavy sound. When the conductor jumps out of the hoop, the class is silent.

2. Variation: Place four hoops in the middle of the room. The class is divided into four "families"—nature sounds, human sounds, man-made sounds, and animals sounds. Each family of sound is guided by one of the hoops. The conductor jumps in and out of the four hoops at random. The "families" follow the conductor and respond only for their hoop.

Pass It On

Concepts: Exploring the natural development of a musical idea.

Materials: Tone bars, vocal sounds, or any other musical sounds.

Ages: 9 and up.

Some melodies seem to have a natural flow to them, as explored in this activity.

1. Divide the class into two groups. One group performs while the other critiques.

2. Each performer gets two pitches or sounds. Appoint a conductor who will indicate to the first player the moment to begin improvising a musical line using only the two pitches. The player continues until the conductor indicates the next person to begin. This new player must use a motif or musical idea presented in the previous melodic line. There should be no pause between the players, so the first player continues until the second player begins. This process continues until each player has had a chance to perform.

3. Ask the following questions of the group that has been observing:

   "Were there repeated ideas?"

   "Did the music flow from one player to the next?"

   "Was there too much repetition? Too much contrast?"

   The observing group then makes a few suggestions to the performing group, and the performers try again.

4. Everyone switches roles and repeats the above process.

5. Variation: The concept of this exercise is to become involved in the organic development of a musical idea. As in a story, music relies on what happens before, with each idea growing out of the previous idea. That is the reason for repetition. Much of the music of Johann Sebastian Bach is very organic, with his musical ideas growing out of simple motifs and patterns. You might want to play his "Prelude" from the *Partita for Solo Violin BWV 1001* (see references at the end of this chapter). Point out to students how the melodic line keeps evolving from the previous material, creating a sense of several ideas but just one musical line.

What Did You Say?

Concepts: Revealing how musical phrases balance and complement each other.

Materials: Sound sources—found sounds, body sounds, vocal sounds (for each student).

Ages: 10 and up.

A common musical phrase will be four measures long: a two-measure statement and a two-measure response. For example: "Twinkle twinkle little star" (statement); "how I wonder what you are" (response).

1. In pairs, one student creates an eight-beat rhythm pattern using their sound. The other student answers with a pattern that complements the first one but is slightly different. For instance:

2. After practicing this idea so that the phrases sound balanced and comfortable, students "converse" with each other, taking turns questioning and answering. This concept can be extended to a study of the "talking drums" of Africa.

Time's Up

Concepts: Exploring organizational tools for composition.

Materials: Clock with second-hand, tape recorder.

Ages: 10 and up.

You can organize this piece by simply putting a time limit on the exercise.

1. The class decides on a unison pitched sound (for instance, singing "la"). Every five seconds, each student changes something in the sound (length, volume, timbre, expressiveness) but not the actual pitch. Continue the piece for thirty seconds.

2. Tape the piece and listen for the repetition ("la") and the contrasts (lengths, volume, etc.). Try several times, each one improvised, so they are all different.

3. The class decides on a rhythmic pattern like:

Every five seconds, each student changes something in the pattern (pitch, sound source, volume, tempo), but not the pattern. Continue for thirty seconds and tape the patterns as above.

Composition

Composition differs from improvisation in that the product is meant to be heard again. Unlike improvisation, this requires a system of notation. A compositional activity can extend an improvisational idea. A musical composition, like a story, has a beginning, middle, and end. It uses the organizing tools of repetition and contrast and might focus on a particular musical element as in an *absolute* composition. An absolute composition is one in which the structure, use of musical elements, and controls is of primary importance. A *programmatic* composition is one in which an extra-musical idea is conveyed through music. The collaborative experiences are of the latter. Of course, in listening to an absolute composition, one can imagine pictures, stories, or ideas that the music might suggest to the listener (see chapter 1). And, of course, a programmatic piece of music has organization and structure that can be analyzed.

Melodic Maneuvers

Concepts: Exploring how to enhance a line of music.

Materials: Paper, markers or pencils, pitched sound source.

Ages: 8 and up.

This compositional activity extends the introductory melodic activity, "Melody Mix-Up," in chapter 2. Melodies can be enhanced in various ways, such as changing amplitude (volume) or timbre (tone color), or adding silence. Students are ready to create their own melodies and notate them. Teachers may give students the following instructions:

1. Find your own sound source. It must be pitched. You can use your voice, tuned water glasses, a xylophone, a glockenspiel, or an orchestral instrument such as piano or flute.

2. Draw a line. You have just notated the melody. Don't worry about actual pitches for the moment—just the overall contour. Play.

3. Draw again. Change the volume in places by shading. Play. The thicker the lines, the louder the volume.

4. Draw again. This time change the tempo by changing the line length (longer line—slower, shorter line—faster). Play.

5. Now add silences. Play. What does this do? It adds rhythm, which is a built-in part of a melody. A rhythm can be without a melody, but a melody cannot be without rhythm. Adding silences also removes the sliding and indeterminate pitch quality of the piece.

6. Variation: Play these three musical selections, which are solo melody pieces: "Syrinx" (flute) by Claude Debussy, "Prelude" from the *Partita for Solo Violin BWV 1001* by Johann Sebastian Bach, and any Gregorian chant (voice). As students listen, ask them to imagine how each selection would look as a line drawing. Have students use butcher paper or adding machine tape and draw the melody as they listen.

Two Lines Are Better Than One

Concepts: Exploring polyphony.

Materials: Chalkboard, pitched and unpitched musical sounds.

Ages: 10 and up.

This activity uses three musical lines. Two melodic lines are in opposition to each other, yet sound simultaneously. This is called counterpoint. The third line is an accompanying line, an ostinato, or repeated pattern. When there are two or more lines together, the composition becomes more complex. We call this kind of music *polyphonic* (poly = many, phonic = sound). The music in this activity is moving away from the impulsiveness of improvisation toward the more controlled structure of composition. Therefore, other controls are added.

1. Draw three musical lines on the board as in the figure below.

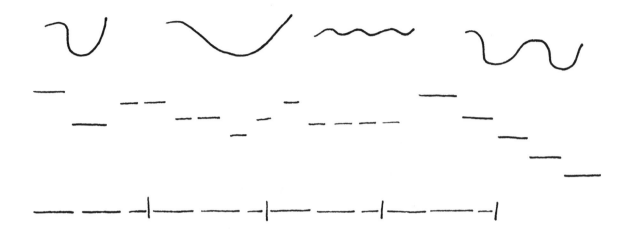

The upper two melodic lines can be played by any pitched instrument. The ostinato pattern (lower line) can be a simple, repeated rhythm performed by body, found, or percussion sounds.

2. Add a time length to the piece, dividing the line into five-second sections.

3. A conductor can now follow the line to give a general indication of the time. The conductor watches a clock and gestures at each five-second time segment.

Here is a summary (from the previous two activities) of the steps for transforming a simple melodic "line" into a composed polyphonic piece:

a. Draw a simple curved line.
b. Manipulate it through various controls (volume, timbre, silence).
c. Add rhythms.
d. Combine one or more lines.
e. Give it a time limit.
f. Add a conductor to hold the piece together.

4. Variation: "Jesu Joy of Man's Desiring," by Johann Sebastian Bach, is an effective and clear example of a polyphonic composition consisting of three musical lines. There are two melodies—the chorale tune and the instrumental obbligato—and a harmonic accompaniment. As students listen to this piece, have them "notate" the individual lines and how they move by drawing lines on pieces of butcher paper that reflect the musical lines. The class can work in groups of three, with each member of a group taking a line.

Theme and Variations

Concepts: Experimenting with variation technique.

Materials: Sound sources—found sounds, body sounds, vocal sounds; paper; markers.

Ages: 10 and up.

Varying a theme (theme and variations) is a standard musical form that has been used by composers for hundreds of years.

1. Have the class create a melody of distinct pitches (highs and lows) and rhythm. Notate with circles, triangles, and other shapes; different shapes describe different sounds/ timbres (e.g., circle = "oooh"; triangle = "eeee"). You can also indicate length of sounds by size. The following is an example of a theme:

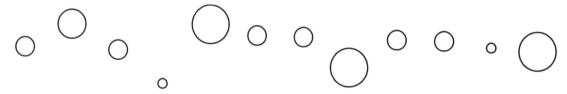

2. Have the class decide how the melody will vary. Again, the lines will reflect how the theme is varied. The following are a few examples of how one can vary a melody:

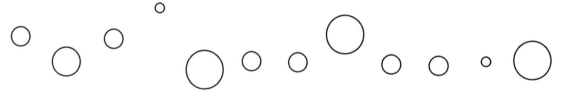

Change in direction/pitch.

Change in length/rhythm.

Change in sound/timbre.

3. To perform, conduct the melody by pointing to each shape for students to follow. Place a slight pause between each variation. See "Musical Maps" below for listening ideas regarding theme and variations.

MUSICAL MAPS

Musical maps are devices that assist the listener in comprehending various structural and organizational elements found in a piece of music. Unlike the responding activities in chapter 1, these musical maps look at specific musical controls and their use rather than the total effect of the composition. Of course, it is all these individual elements that collaborate to create the musical meaning of the work.

Musical maps require a more advanced understanding of music and its compositional structure and might be best used by the music specialist. These maps extend students technical understanding of a piece of music. Musical maps are an effective means of collaborating the compositional and improvisational activities directed by a classroom teacher with these comprehensive listening activities presented by the music specialist. With musical maps, the music specialist can show how composers manipulate these same musical elements and controls students have worked with.

Musical map worksheets, which may be photocopied for each student, are found on pages 81-86. Details for each map follow below. The following are teacher guidelines for using musical maps in listening activities:

1. Tell the class what to listen for. Identify the phrases, meter, or other important musical elements that you want students to hear. Divide the music into sections, if appropriate.

2. Decide which elements are most critical for understanding the piece. Have students concentrate on listening for only one element or control at a time.

3. Discuss directions and the map carefully with students before the music begins. While music is playing, limit talking to only calling off the number identifying the place in the music. After the music is finished, discuss answers. Play again to reinforce.

4. Choose musical selections carefully. If a piece is too long, play just a representational portion.

Musical Map A
Log Sheet

This musical map gives the listener an overall sense of the music. As the piece is playing for the first time, the listener circles and notes anything of particular interest about the music. This map is a good introduction for any piece that the class will study in detail.

Musical Map B
Comparative Listening

Each of these listening charts stresses one or two specific musical elements and how they are treated in contrasting musical examples. Choose parts of several musical selections from the suggestions below or perhaps pieces you are planning to use in further activities. Fill in the names of the selections in the blanks. Students listen to each example and write down a few characteristics or descriptions for each column.

Melody Examples:

Vocalise, op. 34, no. 14 (Rachmaninoff)

"Marriage of Figaro" overture, from *The Mozart Collection* (Mozart)

Sonata for Flute and Piano, first movement (Poulenc)

"Dances of the Ancient Earth," from *Ancient Voices of Children* (Crumb)

Symphony no. 2 in D, op. 43, fourth movement (Sibelius)

Any Gregorian chant

Rhythm Examples:

Unsquare Dance (Brubeck)

"Dance of the Adolescents," from *The Rite of Spring* (Stravinsky)

Ronde, from *The Danserye* (Susato)

Moto Perpetuo, op. 11 (Paganini)

Pine apple Rag (Joplin)

Harmony and Texture Examples:

"Chester" from *Hymns and Fuguing Tunes* (Billings)

"La Réjouissance," from *The Royal Fireworks Music* (Handel)

"Take the A Train" from *Digital Duke* (Ellington)

Any Gregorian chant

Five Pieces for Orchestra, op. 10, any movement (Webern)

Serenade no. 10 in B-flat Major, K.361, any movement (Mozart)

"El Niño busca su vox," from *Ancient Voices of Children* (Crumb)

Musical Map C
Meter Recognition

An actual musical map is not used for this experience, just a blank piece of paper. The emphasis in this kind of listening experience is on the rhythmic meter of the selection. The piece must have a consistent, rhythmic beat, either in duple or triple meter. The steady, unchanging rhythm of the piece should be the prevailing element. Listening to the music in this fashion, the listener becomes aware of the overall organization of the piece through its rhythmic character. One also becomes aware of the phrasing.

First, the teacher must listen to the music and count the exact number of measures in the piece. Each student has a blank piece of paper (adding machine tape works well) and uses a three-lined figure (triangle) to represent triple meter or a two- or four-lined figure (square) to represent a duple meter. As they listen to the selection, students draw the appropriate figure for each measure of the music. They may change their figure if they wish.

After listening, have students count the number of figures they made. The second listening experience is to group the figures into phrases. As students listen, they should make a slash at the completion of each phrase of music. This will help students understand the organizing process.

Suggested Musical Examples:

(Warning—Be aware of pickups to the melody.)

Brandenburg Concerto no. 2 BWV 1047, first movement (Bach) (duple meter)

Any march by Sousa (duple meter)

Symphony no. 8 in B, D.759, from *Unfinished*, first movement (Schubert) (triple meter)

Eine Kleine Nachtmusik, first movement (Mozart) (duple meter)

Musical Map D
Theme and Variations

Three suggestions are presented here for active listening with a theme and variations piece. Theme and variations is an excellent tool for understanding musical structure and organization. Earlier in this chapter, the compositional activity "Theme and Variations" gave ideas on composing a theme and variations piece. In conjunction with this activity, have students listen to how composers from various times treat this musical form.

Version 1

There is no sample map for this version. On a sheet of paper, draw and number squares representing the theme and variations, as many squares as there are sections in the music. Write the number of each section in each box. Divide the class into small groups, each no bigger than the number of boxes. Each student is assigned to one numbered box that corresponds to the theme or one of the variations. As students listen quietly, they draw, when it is their turn, anything they wish that represents what they think is happening in the music. Stop the music after each section so that students can pass the paper to the next person in their group. Do this for the entire piece of music. Next, give students the opportunity to discuss within the group their individual visual responses to the music. Are there any recurring lines, shapes, or colors that relate to more than one section? Then compare all the groups for similarities. This way of responding to a music selection begins with students understanding of the music through their visual responses, which then become a reference for musical language.

Version 2

With this map, for each variation, the listener checks what happens in the music. Comments can be added.

Version 3

This musical map is based on chronological questions regarding what students are hearing.

Suggested Musical Examples:

"Variations on a Shaker Theme," from *Appalachian Spring Suite* (Copland)

Concerto for Orchestra, second movement (Bartok)

"Variations on Ah! vous dirai-je, maman," (Mozart)

"Symphony no. 94 in G, Surprise Symphony," second movement (Haydn)

"The Trout," from *Quintet in A for Piano and Strings,* fourth movement (Schubert)

MUSICAL MAP A

Log Sheet

Directions: Circle the answer that best fits the musical piece you hear. Add any comments that you can about the music.

Piece: _____

Sound (timbre): Brass   Woodwind   String   Percussion   Voice   Electronic   Other

Number Playing: One   Few   Many

Rhythm: Regular Pattern   Irregular Pattern   Changing Pattern

Rhythm: Strong Beat   Weak Beat   Changing Accent

Melody: Angular   Flowing

Melody: Many Pitches   Few Pitches

Texture: Thin   Thick   Changing

Other Characteristics:

From *One Voice: Music and Stories in the Classroom.* © 1995. Teacher Ideas Press. (800) 237-6124.

MUSICAL MAP B

Comparative Listening: Melody

Directions: As you listen to examples from the following four pieces, indicate in the appropriate columns what you hear.

Length	*Movement*	*Contour*
short/long	lyrical/angular	describe with a line

Piece A:

Piece B:

Piece C:

Piece D:

MUSICAL MAP B

Comparative Listening: Rhythm

Directions: As you listen to examples from the following four pieces, indicate in the appropriate columns what you hear.

Meter	*Tempo*	*Note Values*	*Strength*
duple/triple/ changing	fast/slow/ changing	long/short/ combinations	weak/strong/ syncopation

Piece A:

Piece B:

Piece C:

Piece D:

MUSICAL MAP B

Comparative Listening: Harmony and Texture

Directions: As you listen to examples from the following four pieces, indicate in the appropriate columns what you hear.

	Thin/ Thick	Monophonic/ Homophonic/ Polyphonic	Tonal/ Atonal	Melody & Accompaniment	Full Chordal Sound
Piece A:					
Piece B:					
Piece C:					
Piece D:					

MUSICAL MAP D

Theme and Variations: Version 2

Directions: As you listen, use check marks to record what happens during the theme and each variation.

	No Change	*Melody Changes*	*Something Is Added*	*Rhythm Is Altered*	*Timbre Changes*
Theme:					
Variation 1:					
Variation 2:					
Variation 3:					
Variation 4:					
Variation 5:					

MUSICAL MAP D

Theme and Variations: Version 3

Directions: Circle or supply answers to questions during the theme and each variation.

Music: "Variations on a Shaker Theme" from *Appalachian Spring Suite* (Copland)

1. Theme:

   How many instruments play in the melody?

   one   few   many

   What instrument(s) do you hear playing the melody?

   Is there a counter melody or a simple accompaniment beneath the melody?

2. Variation 1:

   This variation is faster or slower than the original theme?

   Which family of instruments plays the melody?

   brass   percussion   strings   woodwinds

3. Variation 2:

   What happens to the theme?

   Can you name the two instruments playing the theme?

   This variation is heard in canon. The second entrance is played by two more instruments. In this variation, is the texture of the music thicker or thinner?

4. Variation 3:

   Is this slower or faster than the second variation?

   Describe the change in character.

   Why does this occur?

   Think of the orchestration, articulation, tempo, texture. Assign a color to this variation.

5. Variation 5:

   The theme is augmented. How many instruments are playing the theme?

   one   few   all

COLLABORATIVE ACTIVITIES

Chants of a Lifetime

Concepts: Exploring rhythmic patterns.

Materials: Paper, pencils, material from another class subject.

Ages: 6 and up.

Rap might be passé, but rhythmic chants are fun and catchy. Not only are they good exercises to improve rhythmic competency, but they are effective ways to remember lists of words that need to be memorized. If your students are memorizing presidents, science vocabulary, historical dates, or whatever, try this method.

1. Display the list of words. Now have the class figure out the rhythm of each word. You do not have to use traditional notation, but it does make this activity easier and also helps to teach rhythmic notation. Once the rhythm of the words is determined, add silences between words or even syllables for rhythmic interest. Practice chanting until everyone is in unison.

2. After the basic chant is learned, vary the volume (soft or loud, gradually or suddenly) and pitch (high or low voice).

3. Try chanting in a round, with one group starting about four beats after the first. Chant several times.

4. Explore the chant polyphonically, adding extra lines. This is especially good for older students. Add a slow-moving bottom part, using new words or the same. Add a very quick, short line for interest.

Picture This

Concepts: Exploring the collaboration of painting, words, and sounds.

Materials: Paper; pencils; various rhythm instruments, pitched instruments, or found sounds; postcards of abstract paintings (available from museum bookstores).

Ages: 10 and up.

This activity involves both composition and notation and also is an effective integrated arts experience. To add another dimension, the groups can incorporate movement to enhance the finished piece.

1. Divide students into small groups. Give each group a postcard of a painting, along with a group of sound sources. Do not reveal the title of the painting to the group at this time.

2. Instruct students to look at their painting and write down a series of adjectives that describe the painting. The words can reflect their various reactions to the work, what they see, or any other connection.

3. Students then determine how they can express these words and images as musical sounds. Would the sounds be loud, soft, fast, slow? Many or few sounds? Would the lines be graceful and smooth or sharp and angular, or a combination? Would the music be free or patterned? Encourage students to experiment with various musical ideas.

4. Next, the adjectives and the music are combined in a manner that the group chooses. They might wish to notate their compositions. They can use symbols, icons, whatever, so they can remember how the piece fits together.

5. Each group performs for the class. The class looks at the paintings and determines which was the inspiration for each composition. Then the original title is revealed. Compare the artists' titles with students' compositions.

Sound Carpets

Concepts: Heightening and broadening the meanings of words.

Materials: Poems (see "Poetry Anthologies" in appendix A); paper; pencils; various rhythm instruments, pitched instruments, or found sounds.

Ages: 10 and up (modified for younger groups).

Sound carpets are wonderfully effective for catching a mood or essence of the written word. Haiku and other short poetic forms are excellent for upper elementary and older students to use for this activity. Younger students can use simpler poems and create sound carpets as a class project.

1. Divide the class into small groups. Each group chooses a poem. Ask groups to do the following: Determine the meaning, character, mood, effect, or feeling the words are portraying. Is it jealousy? Fear? Joy? Indifference? This aesthetic feeling will be conveyed through musical sounds. Now consider the rhythm of the words. Are they free flowing or rhythmic? Is there a specific pulse (accent) that recurs? What is the overall tempo of the poem? Is it fast-paced or relaxed? All these should be considered before students begin their sound carpet.

2. After students determine the mood, character, and tempo of the piece, ask them to observe the overall structure. Are there words or phrases that repeat? Is it more prose-like, without any obvious patterns? This structural element will help in organizing the sounds.

3. Have students choose sound sources. Again, found sounds, body sounds, rhythm instruments, or orchestral instruments can be used. If one person accompanies, only one sound or instrument might be used. This activity is good for pairs; one reading and the other creating the musical sounds. Or, a group might accompany one poem so that several musical lines or ideas can occur. Ask students to choose sound sources that are in character with the words. They must also decide how the sounds will weave into the words. Will they alternate or be simultaneous? Will certain words be punctuated by a specific sound? When words repeat, will sounds repeat?

4. Ask students to determine whether the poem ends loud or soft. Does it change moods at all? These are all aesthetic, analytical questions that should be pursued.

5. Now to notate: Musical notation, like any language, is used as a means to remember. Students do not need to know traditional musical notation unless they have written a melody with specific pitches. Most students will figure out their own notation using symbols they choose. Shapes and lines are perfectly acceptable. Specific directions can be added. The size, color, or quality of the symbol can indicate volume.

NOTES

1. Yehudi Menuhin and Curtis W. Davis, *The Music of Man* (Toronto: Methuen, 1979), 2.

2. Patricia Shehan Campbell, "Unveiling the Mysteries of Musical Spontaneity," *Music Educators Journal* (December 1991): 21.

REFERENCES

Recordings

Bach, Johann Sebastian. *Brandenburg Concerto no. 2 BWV 1047*. Marlboro Festival Orchestra. Casals. CBS MLK-39442 (CD); MT-39442 (cassette).

———. "Jesu Joy of Man's Desiring," from *Bachs Greatest Hits*. RCA 60828-2-RG (CD); 60828-4-RG6 (cassette).

———. Prelude, from *Partita for Solo Violin BWV 1001*. Milstein. Deutsche Grammophon CD-423294-2 GCM2 (CD).

———. Prelude, from *Partita for Solo Violin BWV 1001*. Heifetz. RCA Gold Seal 7708-2 RG (CD); 7708-4 RRG 13 (cassette).

Bartok, Bela. *Concerto for Orchestra*. New York Philharmonic Orchestra. Boulez. CBS MK-37259 (CD); MYT-37259 (cassette).

Berg, Alban. *Three Pieces for Orchestra, op. 6*. London Symphony Orchestra. Abbado. Deutsche Grammophon 423238-2 GC (CD).

Billings, William. "Chester," from *Hymns and Fuguing Tunes*. Gregg Smith Singers. Premier Recordings PRCD-1008 (CD).

Brubeck, Dave. *Unsquare Dance*. Columbia Records SLPX 2177 (LP).

Copland, Aaron. *Appalachian Spring Suite.* Los Angeles Philharmonic Orchestra. Bernstein. Deutsche Grammophon 431048-2 GBE (CD); 431048-4 GBE (cassette).

Crumb, George. *Ancient Voices of Children.* Contemporary Chamber Ensemble. Elektra/Nonesuch 79149-2 (CD); N5-71255 (cassette).

Debussy, Claude. "Syrinx," from *Music of Debussy.* Galway, flute. RCA RCD1-7173 (CD); HREI-7173 (cassette).

Ellington, Duke. "Take the A Train," from *Digital Duke.* GRP Records GRD-9548 (CD).

Gemini. *Rhythmically Moving.* High/Scope Educational Research Foundation M2201-2209 (CD); M2001C-M2009C (cassette); M2001-M2009 (LP).

Gregorian Chants. Benedictine Monks of the Abbey of St. Maurice and Saint-Maur. Philips 432506-2 (CD).

Gregorian Chants. Schola Antiqua. LOiseau-Lyre 425114-2 (CD).

Gregorian Chants. Treasury of Early Music, vol. 1. Haydn Society Records 79038 (CD).

Handel, George Frideric. "Le Réjouissance," from *The Royal Fireworks Music.* New York Philharmonic Orchestra. Boulez. CBS MYK-38480 (CD); MYT-38480 (cassette).

Haydn, Franz Josef. *Symphony no. 94 in G, Surprise Symphony.* Vienna Philharmonic Orchestra. Bernstein. Deutsche Grammophon 431034-2 GBE (CD); 431034-4 GBE (cassette).

Hooked on Classics, vols. 1 and 2. K-tel 6051-4 (cassette) 6051-2 (CD). Note: There are several other *Hooked on Classics* titles recorded on K-tel.

Joplin, Scott. *Pine apple Rag.* Albright. Music Masters 7061-2-C (CD).

———. "Pine apple Rag," from *The Entertainer.* Cornil. Biograph BCD-101 (CD).

Masterpieces of Music Before 1750: An Anthology of Music. Vol. 1: "Gregorian Chant to J. S. Bach." Haydn Society Records CD-7-9038 (CD).

Mozart, Wolfgang Amadeus. "Marriage of Figaro" overture, from *The Mozart Collection.* The City of London Sinfonietta. American Gramophone AGCD-586 (CD); AGC-586 (cassette).

———. "Marriage of Figaro" overture, from *Mozart Weekend.* London Weekend Classics 425513-2 LC (CD).

———. *Serenade no. 10 in B-flat Major, K.361.* Orchestra of the 18th Century. Barenboim. Philips 422338-2PH (CD); 422338-4PH (cassette).

———. "Serenade no. 13 in G, K.525, Eine Kleine Nachtmusik," from *Compact Mozart* (disc 1). Sony Classical 5 SBK 45977 (CD).

———. *Serenade no. 13 in G, K.525, Eine Kleine Nachtmusik.* Vienna Mozart Ensemble. Boskovsky. London 425874-2 LC (CD); 411846-4 LT (cassette).

———. *Variations on "Ah! Vous dirai-je maman," K.265.* Eschenbach. Deutsche Grammophon 429808-2 GMM (CD); 429808-4GMM (cassette).

Paganini, Niccolo. *Moto Perpetuo, op. 11.* NBC Symphony. DellArte DA9020 (CD).

Penderecki, Krystoff. *Threnody for the Victims of Hiroshima.* Polish Radio and TV Symphony. Kawalla. Conifer CDCF-168 (CD); MCFC-168 (cassette).

Poulenc, Francis. *Sonata for Flute and Piano.* Rampal. Odyssey YT-33905 (cassette).

———. *Sonata for Flute and Piano.* Snowden. Virgin Classics VC790846-2 (CD); VC790846-4 (cassette).

Rachmaninoff, Sergei. *Vocalise, op. 34, no. 14.* Scottish National Orchestra. Murphey. Chandos CHAN-8476 (CD); ABTD-1187 (cassette).

Schubert, Franz. *Symphony no. 8 in B, D.759, Unfinished.* Berlin Philharmonic. Barenboim. CBS MK-39676 (CD) 1MT-39676 (cassette).

———. "The Trout," from *Quintet in A for Piano and Strings, D.667.* Budapest String Quartet. Sony Classical (Essential Classics) SBK-46343 (CD); SBT-46343 (cassette).

Sibelius, Jean. *Symphony no. 2 in D, op. 43.* New York Philharmonic Orchestra. Bernstein. CBS MYK-38477 (CD); MYT-38477 (cassette).

Sousa, John Philip. *Band of the Grenadier Guards.* London Weekend Classics 430211-2 LC (CD); 430211-4 LC (cassette).

Stravinsky, Igor. "Dance of the Adolescents," from *The Rite of Spring.* Boston Symphony. Monteux. RCA (Papillion Collection) 6529-2-R6 (CD); 6529-4-RC (cassette).

Susato, Tielman. *Hits of 1500.* Augsburg Early Music Ensemble. Christophous CD-74572 (CD).

Telemann, Georg Philipp. "Réjouissance," from *Suite in A for Flute and Strings.* Madeira Festival Orchestra. Newman, flutist. Vox/Turnabout PVT 7185 (CD); PCT 7185 (cassette).

Webern, Anton. *Five Pieces for Orchestra, op. 10.* London Symphony Orchestra. Dorati. Mercury (Living Presence) 432006-2 (CD).

Books

Allen, Pamela. *Bertie and the Bear.* New York: Coward-McCann, 1983.

Asch, Frank. *Happy Birthday, Moon.* Englewood Cliffs, N.J.: Prentice-Hall, 1982.

Brown, Marcia. *Once upon a Mouse.* New York: Scribners, 1981.

Carle, Eric. *The Secret Birthday Message.* New York: HarperCollins, 1972.

Gag, Wanda. *Millions of Cats.* New York: Coward-McCann, 1928.

Galdone, Paul. *The Little Red Hen.* New York: Clarion Books, 1985.

Hobson, Sally. *Chicken Little.* New York: Simon & Schuster, 1994.

Marshall, James. *Red Riding Hood.* New York: Dial, 1987.

McGovern, Ann. *Too Much Noise.* Illustrated by Simms Taback. Boston: Houghton Mifflin, 1967.

Rockwell, Anne. *The Old Woman and Her Pig and 10 Other Stories.* New York: Thomas Y. Crowell, 1979.

———. *The Three Bears & 15 Other Stories.* New York: Thomas Y. Crowell, 1975.

Sawyer, Ruth. *Journey Cake, Ho!* Illustrated by Robert McCloskey. New York: Viking Press, 1982.

Sendak, Maurice. *Where the Wild Things Are.* New York: Harper & Row, 1963.

Stewig, John, trans. *The Fisherman and His Wife.* Illustrated by Margot Tomes. New York: Holiday House, 1988.

Troughton, Joanna. *Mouse Deer's Market.* New York: Peter Bedrick Books, 1984.

White, E. B. *Charlotte's Web.* New York: Harper & Row, 1952.

4 Uncovering Hidden Stories and Music

Empowering the imagination—that is what the arts are all about. The composer and the writer imagine sounds or stories and commit them to paper. Performers transform these "fly specks and chicken scratches" into inspiring music and storytelling. Listeners and readers again recreate the musical or story experience in meaningful ways.

The experience does not end there, however. The beauty of the arts is their ability to assume many different meanings. Each time you hear a story or a piece of music, you can discover something new. It is in the act of *re*-creating that we create. This transformation, or discovery of new meanings, is an aesthetic element of a work of art. Unlike a mathematical formula, which has the same meaning for each perceiver, an artwork is constantly transformed each time it is experienced. The work of art itself does not change—*you* change as you experience it in different ways. We can move inside what we hear, see, and read to discover new meanings and ideas in music and stories.

This chapter will help teachers to uncover hidden stories and music in the texts you are using. It is a guide to looking at a story or a piece of music differently, to introducing or extending the experience of a particular piece. Using words and sounds, instruments and illustrations, drama and art materials, teachers and students can engage in the delight of discovery. In some cases, these activities are similar to those in earlier chapters, but here there is a greater emphasis on empowering the imagination.

INSIDE STORIES

Asking students to "walk around inside stories" encourages them to imagine other aspects of characters' lives—what they may be thinking, what they may be doing during time lapses in the stories, how others may perceive them, what their homes may be like, or how to picture them in alternative ways.

Through imaginative creation of these aspects, students are recreating the story in new ways. Movement, mental imagery, and pictorial representations are all activities that promote further reflection on the story, enriching and adding meanings to the original text. The idea is to stay within the story parameters for the most part. We are not considering what happens before or after the story, although these are certainly worthwhile considerations that can also enrich story understanding. The idea is to choose an event or setting that comes after the beginning of the story and before the end. Nor are we trying to rewrite the story. All inventions should stay true to the original intentions and ambiance of the tale, to characters' behaviors and personalities. These activities are extensions, not alterations, of the story. The imaginative possibilities are endless and will change the way teachers and students experience stories.

How Do You Crown a King?

Concepts: Exploring interior dimensions of a story as a way of enhancing understanding of character, setting, plot, and theme.

Materials: *Where the Wild Things Are* (Sendak).

Ages: 5-7.

This activity is a perfect example of what "walking around inside stories" means. Here, students step into one episode of Max's dream story and invent what might happen when the "wild things" crown Max king. The text simply says, "and made him king of all wild things," with an illustration showing Max sitting imperiously on a grassy mound, with a crown and scepter. How did the actual crowning take place? The following is a suggested sequence of events, easily adaptable for any class.

1. Read or tell *Where the Wild Things Are*, encouraging the audience to be "wild things"—roaring, gnashing teeth, showing claws, and rolling eyes. You may wish to begin by asking students to don their wolf suits like Max wore ("found" under their chairs or behind them on the floor). They are made like pajamas with feet, so students get into them feet first, then zip them up. Then the hat or hood goes on, and the tail is pinned on.

2. After the story, draw the class into the event by saying you have always wondered how the wild things crowned Max king. Suggest that the class find out. Arrange students in a circle and ask what they would say to someone they are about to crown king. Answers will vary from formal to informal: "I crown you king," "Hi, king," or "Now you are king." Select two or three answers and arrange them in a simple chant with a beat: "Hi, king. I crown you king." Repeat several times with the group, then move the circle slowly clockwise in a simple two-step "dance," repeating the chant.

3. "Discover" Max: "Oh, there you are, Max. I'm glad to see you. Would you stand inside the circle?" Similarly, among students, find two train-bearers, a crown-bearer, and a Lord High Chamberlain, explaining that a crowning is a solemn occasion. If your manner is respectful, students will follow suit.

4. Ask students, "Where did we leave the crown the last time we used it?" The word *we* includes the teacher in the experience, which helps establish its reality for younger students. They will know, or, if they need prompting, suggest it may be under that bush, over there. The crown is carried ceremoniously and with respect. Repeat for the king's robe and scepter. These objects are mimed. No need for props.

5. Design the actual crowning as you wish, perhaps a stately procession forming out of the circle with Max and his court last, moving around the room, ending in the circle. Appropriate music may be added. All mimed objects and music should be referred to in the context of "remember how we have always done this." The whole event should be serious and ceremonial.

6. The crowning takes place in the center of the circle: robe first, placed on Max's shoulders by the train-bearers, then the scepter and crown conferred by the Lord High Chamberlain. Attendants bow and resume places in the circle. Finish with the chant and dance, as above.

7. Attendants return the robe, crown, and scepter to their places, and everyone sits down to discuss how they felt about this. This is an important step, to reflect on the experience as a logical extension of the story. Even though the characters, except Max, are "wild things," the activity seems to work better and remain more controlled if students behave as themselves, although there is certainly room for experimentation with this mini-drama.

Around the House

Concepts: Exploring interior dimensions of a story to enhance understanding of plot, character, and setting.

Materials: Stories and books read in the classroom, a variety of art and writing materials (see below).

Ages: 6-12.

This activity promotes imaginative conceptions of characters' lives within and beyond the story itself. The approach is easily applied to a wide range of literature, from simple folktales for younger students to realistic fiction for older students. It is critical, however, that the designs, in whatever form, truthfully reflect the characters' lives. The results may be triumphantly displayed in the classroom, hall, or media center.

Some of the following suggestions are similar to those in the activity "Outside In" (chapter 2). Consult this activity for other ideas to apply here.

1. After students have read or heard the story or book, engage the class in a discussion of one or more of the following "extras" that could logically apply to characters' lives. Students may then represent these ideas in an appropriate visual art format (an illustration, a poster, a book jacket, a menu, a room design, etc.); in writing (letters, diaries, memos); or a combination of these.

2. What mail might these characters receive? Letters from whom? Junk mail? Invitations or announcements? Postcards? The two *Jolly Postman* books by Janet Ahlberg and Allen Ahlberg (see references at end of this chapter) will be helpful here, even for older students. Include a discussion of how the characters might react to this mail. Design various types of mail.

3. What kind of neighbors might these characters have? If these neighbors gossiped with each other, what might they say about the characters? Invent conversations and tape them, experimenting with various voices. Draw cartoon strips of conversations, with outsize balloons for the words. Mobiles made from these balloons will add motion to the words, giving them another dimension.

4. Imagine a trip to a grocery store or supermarket with one character. What would be in the basket when they checked out? What might be their favorite foods? Consider carefully this character's behavior and personality. Would he or she be likely to crave Chinese food? Country cooking? What might be a typical menu for Sunday dinner? For a cookout? Create menus and even a collection of recipes for a cookbook.

5. Design a room for one character. Consider this character's personality and what you imagine its hobbies might be, what pictures might be on the walls, the style of furniture, colors, what books on the shelves. All items should be a true reflection of students' perception of this character. Individual students' work can be compared for somewhat differing perceptions and discussed. These rooms may be not only designed but built and furnished. Use foam core for floor and walls and construct furniture from index cards or tagboard. If this room were a stage set, what scene (in the story or invented) might take place here? A garden or playground are alternate design possibilities.

Meetings

Concepts: Exploring interior dimensions of a story to enhance understanding of characters, events, and setting.

Materials: Collections of folktales and various picture-story books (see below).

Ages: 6-12.

Explore stories from the inside by inviting a character from one story into another. Allowing a character to make a "guest appearance" in another story enlightens students about the host characters, story events, and setting. Asking readers to assume the voices of the characters themselves is more involving and challenging than the common question, "How is the setting in this story (or book) different from the setting in this book?" Students will encounter characters and situations more closely, and, more importantly, will reflect on the meanings and implications of their reading, for both literary and life experiences.

Books cited below are arranged sequentially, from younger to older students.

1. For classes with younger students, begin with *Dear Peter Rabbit* by Alma Flor Ada, a delightful series of letters from and to characters such as Goldilocks, the three bears, Peter Rabbit, Red Riding Hood, the three pigs, as well as characters from other favorite stories. At the end, they all gather at Goldilocks's birthday party. This book suggests an exception to the rule of staying inside the story. Imagine other encounters or events these characters might have (a picnic, a visit to Red Riding Hood's grandmother, helping Mr. McGregor in his garden).

2. Use this book as a model for bringing together other story characters. What if Lazy Jack, crossing the bridge on his way home, encountered the troll who threatened the three Billy Goats Gruff? Suppose Red Riding Hood's grandmother lived in the same woods where the Bremen Town musicians took up residence? Anne Rockwell's collections of folktales are particularly helpful here (see references at the end of this chapter).

3. For third- and fourth-graders, consider transporting the young girl from *Emily*, by Michael Bedard, into Faith Ringgold's *Aunt Harriet's Underground Railroad in the Sky*. How would she survive Cassie's journey northward? What would she say and do, and what would Cassie think of her? Conversely, could Cassie stop in Amherst (a bit off the track, but we are imagining) to visit Emily Dickinson, a contemporary of Harriet Tubman? Would one of Emily's poems enlighten Cassie's life, as happens with Emily's young friend?

4. Keep in mind that these inventions are just that—temporary episodes that are not meant to change or rewrite the original story, only to explore it. Encourage students to reflect on the experience of this activity in the context of the story or stories involved. Have their perceptions of characters changed? Do they see settings more clearly or differently? Point out that writers, like other artists, always have choices in designing a plot. By discussing and arguing why invented episodes would or would not fit the original story, students are engaging not only in higher-level thinking but in the beginnings of literary criticism.

5. What if the Borrowers (from Mary Norton's Borrowers series) stepped into Mrs. Frisby's world? How would they deal with the rats of NIMH? Include Jane Leslie Conly's sequels to Robert O'Brien's *Mrs. Frisby and the Rats of NIMH* (see references at end of chapter). The country settings in both sets of books make a logical starting point.

6. Fantasy involving time travel allows characters to travel from one book to another without undue strain. The magic is already in place. Children from Anne Lindbergh's books, such as *The Hunky-Dory Diary*, might appear in *Tom's Midnight Garden*, by Philippa Pearce. Or, try combining characters from science fiction novels such as *The Giver* by Lois Lowry, and *Nick of Time* by Anne Lindbergh, encouraging students to compare these two sterile societies.

Otherwhere

Concepts: Exploring interior dimensions of a story to enhance understanding of plot, character, setting, and theme.

Materials: Collections or single copies of folktales (see below).

Ages: 8-12.

Walking around inside stories can also mean considering what might happen during time lapses in the story. In many folktales, a year passes in a sentence or two while the protagonist is journeying, or "a long time" passes as a magic object or an elusive character is sought. The same can be said of literary folktales and authored stories. Look for a passage of time. It is important to keep students' inventions within the story to avoid the temptation to turn this into "what happens after the story." This activity should explore interior possibilities. As in other "walking inside" activities, keep events and behavior true to the main story.

1. For story characters who appear, disappear, then return, discuss with the class where the characters might have gone and what they could have been doing. For instance, in *The Paper Crane* by Molly Bang, the character who makes things happen is the mysterious, unnamed "stranger," dressed in old, worn clothing, but with an appealing manner. Who could he be? Where did he come from? What could he have been doing during the months his paper crane was on loan to the restaurant owner? Invent possible scenarios for this time lapse. These possibilities are intriguing writing starters for a piece done purely for fun, or to practice paragraph structure or the use of literary elements. Questions in the following variations can be explored in writing, class discussion, or art projects.

2. Another consideration is what happens during a journey, one of the most ancient as well as most contemporary motifs in folklore and fiction. Journeys or quests may take years or may be much shorter. Either way, the time lapse is intriguing to explore. How does this character survive? What adventures might they encounter? In *The Water of Life* by Barbara Rogasky, for example, there are several journeys by various characters, but the most intriguing time to consider is probably the year that the youngest son spends in the forest, in hiding. We are told nothing of this year, yet it must have been both difficult and exciting—a king's son living alone in the forest.

2. Similarly, in the title story of *East of the Sun and West of the Moon*, retold and illustrated by Kay Nielsen, the courageous heroine engages in a series of journeys to find the lost prince. The time is unspecified; we are told only that it is long and weary. But when the four winds carry her, one journey to the next, she travels quickly. What would it be like to be carried on the back of the North Wind? Consider all aspects of sky travel: temperature, colors, light and darkness, the moon and sun, stars, planets, and so on.

Another Picture

Concepts: Encouraging students to expand their understanding of a story by considering scenes not pictured. Enhancing visual acuity and mental imagery. Experimenting with various art styles and media.

Materials: Various picture-story books (see below), various art materials.

Ages: 6-12.

In this "inside" activity, the teacher asks each student to illustrate a story event not shown in the picture-story book. Picture-story books in which not every event is illustrated will work well for this activity. For intermediate students, the approach can be a serious study of how and why illustrators choose certain events to portray. This could be a time to contact book illustrators through their publishers for phone, e-mail, or letter conversations on this subject.

1. Choose a picture-story book and discuss with the class the illustrator's choices. In *The Widow's Broom* by Chris Van Allsburg, for example, what is the effect of not showing the witch picking up a glowing coal, or making her own fire, or talking to the witch who rescued her? In Nancy Willard's *Beauty and the Beast*, there are fourteen illustrations for fifty-six pages of text. Why were these particular subjects chosen for illustration? There are no right or wrong answers; these were the artists' choices. Students will need to give stories a close reading and reflect before selecting what they would like to illustrate.

2. Students may choose other events from the book or books to illustrate. Ask them to justify their choices, for example: "I want to see what her face looks like," or "I'd like to imagine this house/barn/castle/cave." Students' illustrations need not follow a particular artist's style or medium, although experimenting with collage, for example, or pen and ink, can give them an experience leading to a greater appreciation of the art of illustration. It is important that details such as numbers, colors, sizes, shapes, and so on are consistent with the story. Readers, especially young ones, are disturbed when illustrations are clearly at odds with the text. At the same time, students should be encouraged to add details not mentioned in the story, just as creative book illustrators do, as long as they are logical and possible.

3. Use students' alternate illustrations to imagine other possible "inside" story events, characters' interactions, or alternate settings not described: a meeting, a quarrel, a search, a discovery, a room, a garden, a grove in the woods, an undersea cave, floating on a cloud, and so on. Display the new artwork and episodes with the original book during National Book Week or a special school event.

The Island

Concepts: Enhancing language skills. Developing mapping skills.

Materials: Large sheets of tagboard, poster board, or mural paper; writing
and art materials (see below).

Ages: 9 and up.

Story composing and storytelling are the focus of this activity. Inventing an island country is also the perfect collaborative process for small groups of students. They will tell the story of their island as they explore many matters necessary for a self-contained country to survive and flourish. These islands may develop slowly over weeks and months, or they may be completed in a few days. This activity can easily be adapted for a whole class, although the logistics of working on one map will be easier in small groups.

1. Each group is given a sheet of tagboard or mural paper on which the teacher has drawn the outline of an island. Make the island as large as possible to allow for many details, but allow some area offshore for the sea, its creatures, and ships.

2. Brainstorm with students the things needed to create a country. Items will cover all areas of the curriculum (see below). The island's general geography is sketched in lightly in pencil during planning, then made permanent.

3. Make each map a picture map showing not only towns, mountains, rivers, roads, and so on but also the national costume, native animals, and more. Design a money system, a flag, and stamps. Write a national anthem. Invent the island's history in the form of legends that can be both written and told. What crops do they grow? Do they trade with another society? What is the weather? Form of government? You will want to consider special problems of living on an island. And, of course, what is this country called?

4. Each group's country will be different and should result in spirited presentations. Perhaps once a day or week, students can collaborate on telling their country's stories, adopting the form of government, producing artworks and music for the culture, trading in its money, exploring its topography, caring for its animals, and so forth. Documents may be written, and speeches, forums, or debates may be recorded on audiotape or videotape. A visiting dignitary may bring great news and must be welcomed and fêted. Possibilities for writing projects and oral presentations abound and may easily be linked to curricular subjects and library research.

MORE THAN MEETS THE EAR

As displayed throughout the experiences in this book, the potential for music is everywhere. In this chapter of going beyond, there are several opportunities for diverse explorations of music. Although the concepts of responding through musical maps, organizing sound patterns, and integrating music with other art forms have already been introduced, the following activities *extend* the processes. Note that these exercises might require a little more imagination and creative thinking, two skills that the arts can illuminate better than any other curriculum subject.

Additionally, the music history and world music activities provide information, albeit brief, that can integrate into social studies and history curricula. There are many excellent resource books and recordings for period music and world music. See the references at the end of this chapter and the appendixes for information on specific recordings and sources for recordings.

Orchestrating a Painting

Concepts: Using nonmusical stimuli for sound compositions.

Materials: Reproductions of paintings (better yet, the real thing).

Ages: 5 and up.

A visual work of art can be the creative stimulus for sound exploration. In turn, musical sounds can be organized to represent an aural interpretation of a visual work.

1. Choose a painting with a lot of activity in it. Use a good, large reproduction, or better yet, visit the local art museum. Instruct students to look for as many sounds in the painting as they can find. Have students look at the painting for one minute. Then, have them turn their backs to the painting (or turn the painting around) and ask them what sounds were present in the painting. This is a good exercise for memory retrieval. Practice making all the sounds that are present.

2. Instruct everyone to choose one of the sounds but not to tell anyone what they have chosen. On cue, imagine that the painting comes off the wall, absorbs the class, and comes to life with everyone making their sounds. On cue, the painting goes back on the wall.

3. Variation: To create a more complex sound story with the painting, try the following:

   • Have a conductor indicate individual sound entrances.

   • Create a rhythmic ostinato of some of the sounds. For instance, if there is a horse in the painting, a repeated "clip-clop" in rhythm could be an artist's pattern.

   • Improvise a verbal story with the sounds.

   • Use found and improvised sounds rather than imitative sounds.

4. Variation: For older students, use abstract and nonrepresentational works of art. Have them determine what appropriate sounds best fit the colors, lines, or shapes. Organize as above.

How Well Do You Hear?

Concepts: Enhancing listening skills.

Materials: Various rhythm instruments, found sounds, or body percussion sounds; blindfolds.

Ages: 9 and up.

In this activity, students are challenged to listen carefully to identify sounds.

1. Divide the class into pairs. Each pair chooses one sound. Each pair must have a different sound. If sound choices are limited, then each sound should have certain rhythmic patterns that students can identify. Make sure each pair can play and identify their sound pattern.

2. Blindfold one of the partners in each pair. Line up the blindfolded students in one long line, side by side. The other students stand across from them but not across from their partner. Partners should be as far apart as they safely can be.

3. On cue, students not blindfolded begin making their sounds. If the sound is a certain pattern, make sure they pause between each repetition of the pattern. They continue making the sounds while the blindfolded students listen and follow the sounds to find their partners. This can become very funny. Students making the sounds must stand still. Only the blindfolded students can move. A referee should intervene when there is danger of people colliding.

4. Continue until all partners have matched up via their sounds.

This exercise reveals how little (or, for some, how much) people rely on their sense of hearing. Some hear on the surface; others can distinguish subtle timbres, dynamics, and shadings that require more concentrated and intense listening. Again, this activity demonstrates that there is a lot more to listening than what meets the ear.

A Room in the House

Concepts: Using architectural terms for describing a piece of music.

Materials: Suggested musical selections: *Water Music* (Handel), "Buckaroo Holiday" (Copland), *The Nutcracker Suite* (Tchaikovsky), *English Folk Song Suite* (Vaughan Williams); tape recorders; poster board; colored markers.

Ages: 10 and up.

In the introduction, a definition for music was given: "Music is the house that sounds live in." This activity will literally take students into that house. Though this exercise is similar in many ways to activities in chapter 1 (responding) and chapter 3 (organization and structure), a visual and tangible image evolves from the listening in this activity. The suggested selections all contain several movements to give each group one movement from a larger work.

1. Assign a small group of students to each movement. If possible, tape each movement separately and allow each group to listen to their movement with their own tape recorder.

2. As the group listens, they should think, "If this piece of music were a room in a house, it would be . . ." Have students ask themselves the following or similar questions:

   - What kind of personality does this room have?

   - Does the room have a specific function?

   - What kind of paintings, decorations, and curtains are in the room?

   - What kind of furniture is in this room?

   - What colors are in this room?

   The answers are sparked from listening to the music. A clustering map may help students as they listen. To make a clustering map, simply suggest possible answers and "cluster" them in groups on paper to help formulate responses. Each student can make their own map, or the group can make a map.

3. At this point, each group should have enough descriptions of their room to draw it. Each group receives a poster board to draw their room.

4. Each group shows their room as the class listens to the specific movement or piece. Then, the group explains further, if necessary.

5. Variation: Upon completion of the house, the class creates a real estate advertisement for the house. Each group makes up one sentence of the ad for their room. Find a way to descriptively link all the rooms.

Music Is Everywhere

Concepts: Exploring the uses of music.

Materials: Suggested musical examples (see below), paper, pencils, slides of
artworks, photographs, videotapes.

Ages: 10 and up.

   One role of music is to enhance, when used to accompany a speaker, a political event, or advertisements, for example. During the Persian Gulf War, nightly news programs showed videotapes of activity in that area, accompanied by background music intended to heighten the emotional content of the visuals. Background music in commercials may have nothing to do with the product being sold; instead, the music is used to catch the listener's attention and make the product more appealing.

   Where else can you hear music that has nothing to do with the art of listening? When music is used for its artistic value, as in a travel monologue of Africa accompanied by authentic African folk music, it makes sense. When music is used purely to "catch" someone, it is not used as it is intended to be unless the music was composed for that specific purpose.

Try using the same piece of music in two ways: aesthetically and commercially.

1. Choose a famous piece, such as any of the programmatic pieces listed below, or any works listed from previous activities.

2. Have students use the piece superficially as background for a commercial they create.

3. Now have them use it artistically. Possibilities include choosing music to accompany slides of famous artworks from the same era or the same country as the composer. Another effective combination is for students to find old photos of their grandparents and great-grandparents and combine them with a piece of music from the same era. Programmatic musical works, such as those listed below, are excellent accompaniments to an assembly of slides, pictures, and photos of the same subject.

Composition	Composer	Subject
Grand Canyon Suite	Grofé	Western United States
"Snowflakes Are Dancing"	Debussy	Winter scenes
The Moldau	Smetna	Waterways
The Four Seasons	Vivaldi	Seasons
Woodland Sketches for Piano	MacDowell	Nature
The Planets	Holst	Outer space
Pastorale	Beethoven	Nature

Painting with Sounds

Concepts: Using a nonmusical stimulus for creating sound compositions.

Materials: Postcard reproductions of museum paintings; choice of instrument sounds, found sounds, or body sounds.

Ages: 10 and up.

This is a variation of the activity "Sound Carpets" (for poems) that was introduced in chapter 3. The same principles used to analyze a poem are used here with a painting. Instead of words, students examine colors, lines, subject matter, intensity, and compositional arrangement and come up with an interpretation of the painting's meaning. This interpretation is translated into a musical carpet.

1. Divide class into small groups, with each group having a museum postcard to create a sound carpet.

2. Depending on the style of the artwork, students might create literal (subject-oriented) sound carpets or atmospheric (abstract) carpets. Both are acceptable.

3. Using compositional and improvisational ideas from the activity "Sound Carpets" (chapter 3), students create a musical carpet that is an aural description of the painting. This carpet would capture the mood, feeling, or essence of the painting. Unlike the activity "Orchestrating a Painting" (earlier in this chapter), this work will probably be more free and improvised.

4. Place all postcards on the board. Each group performs its carpet, and the class guesses which postcard it represents.

MUSIC HISTORY

As stated in chapter 3, a map is useful for showing where you have been. It puts the journey into perspective by helping you understand why you are where you are now.

Such is the journey with music. In these activities we have been dealing with the so-called classical music of Western civilization. Viewing the history of music as a road map can help us understand why music may be going in the direction that it is.

A very brief description of the periods of Western music is presented below. At the end of the chapter are listed recordings of representative samples of music from each time period. Other chapters also have musical listening suggestions in their reference sections that would be appropriate for exploration. Each description gives a few important points that highlight the music of that period. Of course, the reference list cannot possibly identify all the music of a particular era.

This section is most appropriate for fourth-grade students and up, depending on which grade students begin to study world history. It will not make much sense to younger students.

Medieval (800-1400): The medieval period, or the Middle Ages, was a time when the church was very influential. Most music was composed for the church and sung simply, with no instrumental accompaniment. Instrumental music was largely folk, improvised, and used simple handmade instruments such as drum, fiddle, and pipe or other crude wind instrument. The social structure played an important role with music. Noblemen either wrote and sang love ballads to their ladies or hired troubadours to sing for them. The music of the serfs was very earthy, mostly dance and simple folk tunes. Most music was improvised and not written down, as music notation was largely unknown. The Gregorian chant of the Catholic Church was probably the most important contribution to music from this time.

Renaissance (1400-1600): This term meaning "rebirth" reflected an overall interest in the physical nature of human beings (humanism) as opposed to the narrow thinking of the medieval period. The Renaissance person was one interested and learned in all intellectual pursuits as well as artistic endeavors. This time is known as the Age of Discovery, with many great explorers, inventors, authors, thinkers, artists, and composers contributing to the culture. An awakened interest in instrumental music was accompanied by the development of instruments. Dance music, vocal music, and church music were enjoyed by everyone from peasants to kings. The role of the composer was gaining in importance. In vocal music, the madrigal was most important. Writing for ensembles featuring a variety of wind, string, and keyboard instruments was popular. Secular music was becoming as important as sacred music, reflecting the basic philosophy of the times.

Baroque (1600-1750): This era was marked by many scientific and technological advancements in music. The major/minor key system was introduced; the orchestra as we define it came into existence; structures and forms in musical composition became standardized; and the importance of the composer was established. Music reflected the times quite vividly. It was a period of change and adventure. There were struggles, clashes, and conquests throughout the world. Artists described these experiences through bold, vigorous, decorative, and monumental works. The music of Johann Sebastian Bach, Henry Purcell, Antonio Vivaldi, and George Frideric Handel reflects great displays of emotions of all kinds, complexity, simplicity, joy, sorrow, and hope. The development of an orchestra with various sounds (winds, strings, percussion) marked the baroque period, and Bach's many compositions established the baroque ideal.

Classical (1750-1820): Reflecting more of the Renaissance ideals, the Enlightenment was the important social movement of this period. Interest in natural morality, individual freedom, equal rights, universal education, and common sense prevailed. The American Revolution and the French Revolution occurred during this period, expressing these social ideals. Likewise, order, balance, and simplicity were the goals of composers during this time, contrasting greatly with the sounds of the baroque period. The symphony orchestra became standard with the works of Wolfgang Amadeus Mozart, Franz Josef Haydn, and Ludwig van Beethoven. Mozart and Beethoven, two of the greatest composers of all time, reflected these classical ideals, although they were near opposites in terms of musical styles and personalities. Beethoven's music, coming near the end of this period, is seen as a bridge to the romantic period.

Romantic (1820-1900): The so-called Age of Progress, signaling the Industrial Revolution, made radical changes in daily life in this era. It affected how people lived, dressed, worked, and enjoyed themselves. The term "romantic" does not refer to love but rather to a philosophy that suggests dramatic conflicts, great changes of moods, wanderlust, and sentimental feelings. The nineteenth century was the age of the composer, the "suffering artist," and the virtuoso musician. Instruments became more sophisticated with the use of machines and advanced tools in manufacturing (e.g., the grand piano). Contrasting with the classical period, the music of the 1800s expressed great emotions, moods, and drama. Much of the music was massive, if not in actual sound and length, then in passion and emotion. Music of all kinds was composed, from solo pieces and sacred pieces to opera and orchestral works.

Twentieth Century (1900-present): If art reflects life, the twentieth century is a perfect example of this philosophy. As the world has become noisier and much more complicated and confusing, so has music, with the "anything goes" concept—a term that well represents this century of music. Experimentation with new instruments, techniques, electronic media, and other ideas makes the music of our time quite diverse and exciting. As people are willing to explore new frontiers in science, medicine, and warfare, so are artists willing to try new sounds, media, forms, and structure. It is difficult, if not impossible, to give only one or two illustrations of twentieth-century music.

Name That Era

Concepts: Determining a musical composition's time period.

Materials: Representative recordings (see references at the end of this chapter), slides or postcards of art works (see below), worksheet with time periods and dates (see the sample worksheet on page 109).

Ages: 9 and up.

This is a good activity to introduce music history to students. It also is a wonderful addition to a history class with older elementary and middle school students. Like the next two activities, it is an excellent way to tie the humanities with historical events.

1. Create a tape with a representative excerpt from each period of music, but not in chronological order. Use the suggested recordings at the end of the chapter or any other appropriate recordings from the different eras. Other listening examples, especially those from "Musical Map B" (see chapter 3), would also be appropriate. The public library should have various recordings.

2. Each excerpt should be about one minute long. Give each student a copy of the worksheet. Play the series of excerpts. Have students draw a line from the example being played to the particular period it represents.

3. After all the excerpts have been played, read off the answers to check students' responses. Again, this is a way to *introduce* music history, not a test!

Dateline: Music

Concepts: Viewing music as a part of history.

Materials: Butcher paper, markers.

Ages: 9 and up.

To incorporate the periods of musical history into the overall history of the Western world, have the class make a timeline, beginning with the ancient Greeks.

1. A long strip of butcher paper is good for this. Divide students into groups, with each working on a time period along the timeline. Each group should have their own piece of paper. Have groups mark off the centuries and the time period on the timeline and include the following topics:

different periods or ages

important wars and battles

kings, queens, and other rulers

authors

explorers

historical events

inventions and discoveries

composers and artists

2. Also on the timeline, have each group draw a person wearing the clothes popular during that time. This helps students get a sense of how music fits into the historical picture.

3. When each group has completed their portion of the timeline, tape all of them together and hang the timeline on a classroom wall.

Artist/Composer: Painting/Music

Concepts: Integrating music and art.

Materials: Slides of various artworks, musical examples (see references at the end of this chapter).

Ages: 10 and up.

This is an excellent way to integrate the visual arts and music. Students will also enjoy the challenge of putting together a multimedia slide show for the class.

1. Obtain slides of various artworks of different eras from an art gallery or museum. Most museums have a gift store that sells slides. Some let teachers borrow from their library. Others have a teacher materials center or packets available that contain various slides.

   If you have difficulty in obtaining slides, locate the excellent series of art postcards titled *Mommy, It's a Renoir!* (any bookstore should be able to order them). They feature a wide variety of artists, paintings, and periods. Pictures can be taken of these postcards and made into slides. If you have access to a videocamera, that would work also.

2. Arrange the slides in chronological order. Then, have students determine the essence of each painting by a simple visual analysis. This will help them decide the best kind of music for the accompaniment. The following are questions to ask about each work of art:

   Are the colors bright? muted? shady? brilliant? mixed?

   Are the lines obvious? subtle? angular? smooth?

Is there a subject with a story, or is it a composition featuring forms, shapes, and lines?

Is there negative space (blank canvas)? Is the canvas crowded? Is there balance between the halves?

Does there appear to be a smooth, bumpy, or mixed texture?

What kinds of paint or other materials were used?

3. Find some musical examples as possible accompaniments from the same historical period as the painting. Play several different examples while students concentrate on the painting. Which selection appears to be most congruous with the visual? If the music is very fast and busy, and the painting is a still life, that probably would not be the best choice of music. A slow, lyrical string passage would probably be more appropriate.

4. Once students have a painting or two for each period and the appropriate musical selections, have them invite other classes to experience their multimedia "culture in a nutshell" show!

MUSIC HISTORY WORKSHEET

Directions: As you listen, draw a line from the example number to the time period that you think the music represents.

Example   *Time Period*

A   Medieval (800-1400)

B   Renaissance (1400-1600)

C   Baroque (1600-1750)

D   Classical (1750-1820)

E   Romantic (1820-1900)

F   Twentieth Century (1900-present)

MUSICAL WORLD MAP

You have just won the lottery! Your dream come true—a trip around the world. What do you do first? That's right, get a map out to decide where you will go.

Having a musical map of the world would not hurt either. Each country or culture has its own musical traditions. Countries take great pride in preserving their folk traditions—especially music.

In the United States, folk music is characterized by a little bit of this country's sound, blended with a little bit of that country's rhythm, mixed with a little of another country's melody, and so on. Just as this nation is a melting pot of cultures from all corners of the world, so is our music. Most musical experts agree that jazz is America's true music, but even jazz has roots in other regions—Africa and Europe.

The traditional music of each country can usually be traced back to that country's beginnings, for most traditional folk music has not changed much through the course of history. That is why it is called "folk" music. Another word for "folk" is "people." Therefore, one could call folk music, "people music." That would imply that it is music for all people. Folk music is meant to represent the people of a culture. It has specific characteristics that distinguish it from classical music.

1. Folk music is usually simple, with repeated melodies, words, and rhythms.

2. Folk music is frequently passed on orally and not always notated, so elements are often changed when passed on.

3. Folk music uses instruments that are generally simple to make and play. Traditionally, folk musicians are not professionally trained musicians. That is not to say they are not talented. They "learn on the job," so to speak.

4. Folk music seldom has specific instrumental or voice choices. It is performed by whatever instrument or singer is available.

Conversely, music in some cultures is subject to certain restrictions, based on symbolism and rituals, that require certain people to perform specific pieces, or some pieces to be performed only at certain times or places. In essence, the music is interwoven with religion or the way people live. Therefore, folk music often plays a far more important role than just being a pastime. Folk music can tell us much about a culture.

For the student, folk music is almost always more accessible than classical music. Though sometimes the songs may strike students as strange when heard in the native language, students should enjoy listening to and learning about many kinds of folk music. Refer to the basic listening suggestions in the introduction and in chapter 3.

World music has really been catching on in the United States in recent years. One excellent source for world music, especially that of Eastern European countries, Israel, and the United States, is the High/Scope Folk Music Series performed by Gemini. They use a variety of instruments indigenous to each country and sing in the native tongue. Their musicality is always top-notch. These recordings are useful for many purposes in learning situations. (See references at the end of chapters and appendixes C and D.)

Younger students who have not begun studying other countries in detail can be introduced to the sounds of a certain country. For instance, if students are being read an African folktale or a Chinese folktale, the teacher can play a musical piece or song from that culture as well.

For older students studying geography, it is natural to include an overview of the music of the country or culture. Students can then do a little research about a specific country's music. When introducing folk music of another culture, a musical map focusing on important aspects of the music is helpful. The "World Music" musical map on page 112 is similar to "Musical Map A" (in this chapter), except that it looks beyond the sound itself to a more holistic examination of the musical selection.

Where in the World?

Concepts: Exploring the music of another culture.

Materials: World music recording (see references at the end of this chapter),
   "World Music" musical map for each student (see below).

Ages: 10 and up.

For further information on recordings, contact Elderly Instruments (see appendix D) for their extensive catalogue of recordings. As in the musical map activities in chapter 3, choose a piece of music and have students fill out the map as they listen. You will need to tell them the name of the piece and its country or region.

MUSICAL MAP

World Music

Piece: _____

Country: _____

1. What was the most prevailing characteristic? **sound   rhythm   melody   tempo**

2. What was the source of the sound?   **instrumental   vocal   both**

   Describe briefly the quality of the sound (high/low, nasal/rich, full/thin, clear/fuzzy, etc.)

3. What was the form of the piece?   **simple   complex**

   Describe briefly one characteristic defining the form (for example, a repeated phrase, got faster and faster, instrumental change every verse, etc.)

4. What is the mood of the piece?   **somber   joyous   neutral**

   Elaborate on what you think its mood reflects. When and where would this music be heard?

5. If possible, do some research on the music of this country. Find out more about what role music plays in this country. Discover if this piece would be a typical piece representing the folk music of this culture. Why or why not?

COLLABORATIVE ACTIVITIES

Orchestrating a Story

Concepts: Exploring the musical parameters of a story.

Materials: Folktale such as *Little Red Riding Hood* (found in Rockwell's *The Three Bears & 15 Other Stories*), rhythm instruments (see below).

Ages: 5 and up.

Just as a visual work of art can be a stimulus for a musical composition, so can a story. The process is similar to orchestrating a painting—choosing characters, sounds, and other important points to express musically. The activity "ECCO Meets Jack—A Sound Story" (chapter 2) is one way a story is orchestrated using found sounds. This activity uses classroom instruments to orchestrate *Little Red Riding Hood* as an example for orchestrating any simple story.

1. Choose an appropriate instrumental sound for each character or part. Consider the following suggestions:

Character	Musical Sound
Red Riding Hood (a unique sound)	Triangle
The Wolf (a loud sound)	Large drum
Grandma (a small sound)	Glockenspiel
The Forest (woods sounds)	Sticks
Cake and Fruit Goodies	Maracas
Eyes (high sound)	Soprano xylophone
Ears (medium sound)	Alto xylophone
Teeth (low sound)	Bass xylophone
Closet (shutting sound)	Cymbals
Hunter	Hand drums

2. Organization is easy—students just play their sound when their character is mentioned as the teacher reads the story.

3. Variation: For a more challenging orchestration, create ostinatos (rhythm patterns) for each character or part. Use tempo and dynamic changes. After each student knows their part well enough, use a conductor to conduct the musical piece without the words. Have another class listen to see if they can guess what story is being orchestrated.

Rosie Revisited

Concepts: Exploring the texture of a work.

Materials: *Rosie's Walk* (Hutchins); found, body, and rhythm instruments sounds.

Ages: 6 and up.

In a three-dimensional visual work, such as a sculpture, the work appears to have more than one surface or way of looking at it. Similarly, polyphony is music that has two or more independent musical lines occurring simultaneously. In a story, there can be more than one character or idea occurring simultaneously. *Rosie's Walk* has a complex texture consisting of two independent lines (the hen and the fox) happening at the same time.

1. Read the story to the group, showing the illustrations.

2. Ask students: "If the hen were a line, what would that line look like?" Elicit answers from students. Ask a student to draw the line on the chalkboard. It should be rather nondescript, with no excitement, just a plain old line.

3. Ask students: "What words would describe the way Rosie (the line) moves?" Suggested answers would probably be "calm," "straight," "casual," and so on.

4. Ask students: "What incidents happen to the fox in the story?" Have students describe each calamity that befalls the fox.

5. Discuss how to describe each of these events with a line or abstract picture. Students volunteer to draw these on the chalkboard.

6. Compare the different lines that represent Rosie and the Fox. Discuss how the story shifts from Rosie to the Fox throughout. This creates the structure of the piece. In contrast to the lines showing story events, the line that represents Rosie is continuous throughout the story. She does not waver. This is analogous to an ostinato in music.

7. Juxtapose the line representing Rosie with each of the incidents involving the Fox. Visually represent this on the chalkboard.

8. Now it is time to add musical sounds to the story. Ask students: "What would be an appropriate sound pattern for Rosie, keeping in mind her line and the way it moves?" The musical pattern should be repetitive, unwavering, and steady.

9. Have students determine sounds that are descriptive of each of the Fox's incidents. They should contrast with Rosie's sounds. Again, these can be found sounds, body sounds, sounds made with rhythm instruments or classical instruments. The fox sounds will probably be loud, non-rhythmic, surprising, and unsteady, to indicate the suddenness of the events.

10. Divide the class. Part of the class is Rosie throughout. Small groups of students can represent each of the catastrophes that happen to the fox.

11. The teacher reads the story while the class performs the musical sounds.

12. Variation: Listen to the musical selection *Children's March: Over the Hills and Far Away* by Percy Grainger. It is a wonderful example of a slow, steady, rhythmic, walking tune, just as Rosie walks.

Beginnings and Endings

Concepts: Exploring the effect of beginnings and endings in story and music.

Materials: Basket of phrases, basket of adjectives, basket of found sounds.

Ages: 10 and up.

We all know the importance of how we begin and end an action. Beginnings and endings are also what listeners or viewers remember most. How a work is received in its first seconds is extremely critical. One wants the listener or viewer to be swept into the piece immediately. In the same way, those last few notes, phrases, or images are what the listener or viewer goes home with and will remember most about the work.

This collaborative activity explores the importance of beginning and ending a work. Using sounds and words collectively heightens the intensity of the experience. In the adjective basket, place words such as *mysterious, calm, frantic, excited, frightened*, and *erratic*. The phrase basket should contain both first lines and last lines. For suggested first lines, see the activity "First Lines" (chapter 3). Last lines are listed as follows:

And the celebration began.

So that was the end of the king who wanted more than anything to touch the moon.

He has been wearing the silver bell round his neck ever since.

He took a wife and lived among his happy people forever and a day.

And then she went forth again in search of her own destiny.

And the dragons are still frightened of him, as if he had a dragon for breakfast every day.

From that day forth, they were greatly honored.

1. Divide the class into small groups. Each group chooses an adjective out of the basket of adjectives. Groups also choose one phrase out of the phrase basket to either begin or end the group's story. Some phrases may be obvious beginnings or endings or may be interchangeable.

2. Out of the "found sounds" basket, each group chooses several sound sources. They may also use what is around and on them. (Suggested found sounds can be located in the chapter 5 activity "Instruments from Junk.")

3. Have students decide whether their phrase is most appropriate as a beginning or ending. They then write the other half.

4. Because the emphasis is on the impact of how a work of art begins and/or ends, the middle is insignificant. The group can write a few lines describing something alluded to in their opening line without developing a complete theme or plot.

5. Have students create a sound carpet or sound effects that keep with the overall feeling suggested by their chosen adjective. The sounds interspersed with the story must complement the words and the adjective. They can be improvised, keeping the general atmosphere, or a composed rhythm.

6. Have groups compose another piece by changing either the beginning or ending phrase, or the adjective.

7. Have each group perform both pieces for the rest of the class. Discuss which piece has the greater impact and why.

The Dancing Conductor

Concepts: Enhancing a sense of story, musical rhythms, and pitch.

Materials: Any poem with a strong rhythm, such as the "Sink Song" in Bob
Barton's *Tell Me Another* (see references at end of this chapter).

Ages: 9 and up.

1. Divide the class into small groups. Each group should have at least two lines of the poem. Give each group a copy of its lines and arrange groups so that the lines will be consecutive when read. Groups should be spread in a circle with as much room as possible in the center.

2. Give each group several minutes to become familiar with the lines. Each group will chant its lines together. The leader (teacher or a selected student) begins dancing the poem in front of one group, making movements as large as possible. The group chants the lines in response to the leader's movements. For example, if the leader jumps and flings his or her arms around, the group will chant loudly and fast, letting voice pitch follow the leader's highs and lows. Similarly for slow movements. Soft sounds may be indicated by arms drawn inward, head lowered, and so on.

3. As soon as one group's lines are done, the leader quickly moves to the next group, perhaps with a slide or a jump, continuing the poem without pause between lines.

4. Variation: The group may chant their lines as "leader," with a person in the center following their voice cues with body movements as above.

5. Discuss with the class aspects of sound, such as why we tend to associate loud with fast and slow with soft. See the activity "The Storm" (chapter 2). What are some circumstances in which loud might be slow or soft might be fast? Use this activity to experiment with passages from stories the class is telling or reading or with story orchestrations such as *Little Red Riding Hood* (see the activity "Orchestrating a Story" in this chapter).

REFERENCES

Recordings

Medieval Music

Gregorian Chants. Benedictine Monks of the Abbey of St. Maurice and Saint-Maur. Philips 432506-2 (CD).

Gregorian Chants. Schola Antiqua. L'Oiseau-Lyre 425114-2 (CD).

Gregorian Chants. Treasury of Early Music, vol. 1. Haydn Society Records 79038 (CD).

Masterpieces of Music Before 1750: An Anthology of Music, vol. 1: "Gregorian Chant to J. S. Bach." Haydn Society Records CD-7-9038 (CD).

Renaissance Music

Italia Mia. The Waverly Consort. CBS MT-36664 (cassette).

Susato, Tielman. *Hits of 1500.* Augsburg Early Music Ensemble. Christophous CD-74572 (CD).

Treasury of Early Music, vol. 2. VO13 Haydn Society Records CD-7 9101 (CD).

Baroque Music

Bach, Johann Sebastian. "Air on a G String," on *Bach's Greatest Hits.* RCA 60828-2 RG (CD); 60828-4 RG6 (cassette).

———. *Brandenburg Concerto no. 2 BWV 1047.* Marlboro Festival Orchestra. Casals. CBS MLK-39442 (CD); MT-39442 (cassette).

———. "Jesu Joy of Man's Desiring," from *Bach's Greatest Hits.* RCA 60828-2 RG (CD); 60828-4 RG6 (cassette).

———. Prelude, from *Partita for Solo Violin BWV 1001.* Milstein. Deutsche Grammophon CD-423294-2 GCM2 (CD).

———. Prelude, from *Partita for Solo Violin BWV 1001.* Heifetz. RCA Gold Seal 7708-2 RG (CD); 7708-4 RRG13 (cassette).

———. *Two Part Inventions BWV 772-786.* Malcolm, harpsichord. Elektra/Nonesuch 71144-4 (cassette).

———. *Two Part Inventions BWV 772-786.* Schiff, piano. London 411974-2 LH (CD).

Baroque Collection. Vox/Turnabout PVTS 7601-C (CD); PCTS 7601 (cassette).

Great Baroque Favorites. CBS MYK-38482 (CD); MYT-38482 (cassette).

Handel, George Frideric. "Le Réjouissance," from *The Royal Fireworks Music.* New York Philharmonic Orchestra. Boulez. CBS MYK-38480 (CD); MYT-38480 (cassette).

Vivaldi, Antonio. *The Four Seasons, op. 8, nos. 1-4.* I Musici. Agostini. Philips 426847-2 PH (CD); 426847-4 PH (cassette).

———. "Winter," from *Solid Gold Baroque.* Vanguard Classics OVC 4021-CED.

Classical Music

Beethoven, Ludwig van. *Symphony no. 6 in F, op. 68, "Pastorale."* Berlin Philharmonic Orchestra. Karajan. Deutsche Grammophon (Galleria) 415833-2 GGA (CD); 415833-4 GGA (cassette).

Haydn, Franz Josef. *Symphony no. 94 in G, "Surprise Symphony."* Vienna Philharmonic Orchestra. Bernstein. Deutsche Grammophon 431034-2 GBE (CD); 431034-4 GBE (cassette).

———. *Trios for Piano, Violin, and Cello.* Beaux Arts Trio. Philips 422831-2 (CD).

Mozart, Wolfgang Amadeus. "Marriage of Figaro" overture, from *The Mozart Collection.* London Sinfonietta. American Gramophone AGCD-586 (CD); AGC-586 (cassette).

———. "Marriage of Figaro" overture, from *Mozart Weekend.* London Weekend Classics 425513-2 LC (CD).

———. *Serenade no. 10 in B-flat Major, K.361.* Orchestra of the 18th Century. Barenboim. Philips 422338-2 PH (CD); 422338-4 PH (cassette).

———. *Serenade no. 13 in G, K.525, "Eine Kleine Nachtmusik,"* from *Compact Mozart* (disc 1). Sony Classical 5 SBK 45977 (CD).

———. *Serenade no. 13 in G, K.525, "Eine Kleine Nachtmusik,"* Vienna Mozart Ensemble. Boskovsky. London 425874-2 LC (CD); 411846-4 LT (cassette).

———. *Variations on "Ah! Vous dirai-je maman," K.265.* Eschenbach. Deutsche Grammophon 429808-2 GMM (CD); 429808-4 GMM (cassette).

Romantic Music

Brahms, Johannes. *Variations on a Theme by Haydn, op. 56a.* Marlboro Festival Orchestra. Casals. Sony Classical SMK 46247-CD; SMT 46247 (cassette).

Grieg, Edvard. *Peer Gynt Suites nos. 1 and 2, op. 46 and op. 55.* Royal Concertgebouw Orchestra. Philips 41158-4 PB (cassette).

MacDowell, Edward. *Woodland Sketches for Piano, op. 51.* Fierro, piano. Elektra/Nonesuch 71411-4 (cassette).

Paganini, Niccolo. *Moto Perpetuo, op. 11.* NBC Symphony. Dell'Arte DA9020 (CD).

Smetna, Bedrich. *The Moldau.* Chicago Symphony. Barenboim. Deutsche Grammophon (Galleria) 415851-2 GGA (CD); 415851-4 GGA (cassette).

Tchaikovsky, Piotr Ilyich. *The Nutcracker Suite, op. 71A.* Suisse Romande. Ansermet. London 417097-4 LT (cassette).

———. *The Nutcracker Suite, op. 71A.* New York Philharmonic Orchestra. Bernstein. CBS MYK-37238 (CD); MYT-37238 (cassette).

Twentieth-Century Music

Bartok, Bela. *Concerto for Orchestra.* New York Philharmonic Orchestra. Boulez. CBS MK-37259 (CD); MYT-37259 (cassette).

Berg, Alban. *Three Pieces for Orchestra, op. 6.* London Symphony Orchestra. Abbado. Deutsche Grammophon 423238-2 GC (CD).

Copland, Aaron. *Appalachian Spring Suite.* Los Angeles Philharmonic Orchestra. Bernstein. Deutsche Grammophon 431048-2 GBE (CD); 431048-4 GBE (cassette).

———. "Buckaroo Holiday," from *Rodeo.* New York Philharmonic Orchestra. Bernstein. CBS MYK-36727 (CD); MYT-36727 (cassette).

Crumb, George. *Ancient Voices of Children.* Contemporary Chamber Ensemble. Elektra/Nonesuch 79149-2 (CD); N5-71255 (cassette).

Debussy, Claude. "Snowflakes Are Dancing," from *Children's Corner Suite.* Ulster Orchestra. Tortelier. Chandos CHAN-8756 (CD); ABTD-1395 (cassette).

———. "Syrinx," from *Music of Debussy.* Galway, flute. RCD1-7173 (CD); HREI-7173 (cassette).

Grainger, Percy. *Children's March: Over the Hills and Far Away.* Central Band of the Royal Air Force. EMI Records CDC 7496082 (CD).

Grofé, Ferde. "Sunrise," from *Grand Canyon Suite.* New York Philharmonic Orchestra. Bernstein. CBS MYK-37759 (CD); MYT-37759 (cassette).

Handel, George Frederick. *Water Music: Suite.* New York Philharmonic Orchestra. Boulez. CBS MYK-38480 (CD) MYT-38480 (cassette).

Holst, Gustav. *The Planets, op. 32.* Berlin Philharmonic Orchestra. Karajan. Deutsche Grammophon 40028-2 GH (CD); 400028-4 GH (cassette).

Penderecki, Krystoff. *Threnody for the Victims of Hiroshima.* Polish Radio and TV Symphony. Kawalla. Conifer CDCF-168 (CD); MCFC-168 (cassette).

Poulenc, Francis. *Sonata for Flute and Piano.* Rampal. Odyssey YT-33905 (cassette).

———. *Sonata for Flute and Piano.* Snowden. Virgin Classics VC790846-2 (CD); VC790846-4 (cassette).

Rachmaninoff, Sergei. *Vocalise, op. 34, no. 14.* Scottish National Orchestra. Murphey. Chandos CHAN-8476 (CD); ABTD-1187 (cassette).

Stravinsky, Igor. *Ebony Concerto for Clarinet and Jazz Ensemble.* Goodman. CBS MK-42227 (CD); MT-42227 (cassette).

Vaughan Williams, Ralph. *English Folk Song Suite.* London Wind Orchestra. Wick. Elektra/Nonesuch N1-78002 (cassette).

Folk Music

Beyond Boundaries. (Various artists). Earthbeat Earthb-CD2552 (CD); Earthb-C2552 (cassette).

Gemini. *Rhythmically Moving.* High/Scope Educational Research Foundation M2201-2209 (CD); M2001C-M2009C (cassette); M2001-M2009 (LP).

Hart, Mickey. *Planet Drum.* Rykodisc RYKO-CD10206 (CD); RYKO-C10206 (cassette).

Instruments. (Various artists). Hannibal HAN-CD 8302 (CD); HAN-C8302 (cassette).

Putmayo Presents: The Best of World Music, vol. 1: World Vocal. Rhino Rhino-CD 71203 (CD); Rhino-C71203 (cassette).

Putmayo Presents: The Best of World Music, vol. 2: Instrumental Music. Rhino Rhino-CD 71204 (CD); Rhino-C71204 (cassette).

United Artists of Messidor. Messidor MESSI-CD 15823 (CD).

World Beat Explosion. (Various artists). Shanachie SHAN-C64008 (cassette).

World Music Sampler. Lyrichord World Music. LYRCD-7414 (CD).

World Music Sampler. (Various artists). Shanachie SHAN-CD9101 (CD); SHAN-C9101 (cassette).

Books

Ada, Alma Flor. *Dear Peter Rabbit.* Illustrated by Leslie Tryon. New York: Atheneum, 1994.

Ahlberg, Janet, and Allen Ahlberg. *The Jolly Christmas Postman.* New York: Little, Brown, 1991.

———. *The Jolly Postman: Or Other People's Letters.* New York: Little, Brown, 1985.

Bang, Molly. *The Paper Crane.* New York: Greenwillow, 1985.

Barton, Bob. *Tell Me Another.* Markham, Ontario: Pembroke, 1986.

Bedard, Michael. *Emily.* Illustrated by Barbara Cooney. New York: Doubleday, 1992.

Conly, Jane Leslie. *Racso and the Rats of NIMH.* New York: Harper & Row, 1986.

———. *RT, Margaret, and the Rats of NIMH.* New York: Harper & Row, 1990.

Hutchins, Pat. *Rosie's Walk.* New York: Macmillan, 1968.

Lindbergh, Anne. *The Hunky-Dory Diary.* New York: Harcourt Brace Jovanovich, 1986.

———. *Nick of Time.* Boston: Little, Brown, 1994.

Lowry, Lois. *The Giver.* Boston: Houghton Mifflin, 1993.

Nielsen, Kay. *East of the Sun and West of the Moon.* Garden City, N.Y.: Doubleday, 1977.

Norton, Mary. *The Borrowers.* First book in The Borrowers series. New York: Harcourt Brace Jovanovich, 1952.

O'Brien, Robert C. *Mrs. Frisby and the Rats of NIMH.* New York: Atheneum, 1971.

Pearce, Philippa. *Tom's Midnight Garden.* New York: J. B. Lippincott, 1958.

Ringgold, Faith. *Aunt Harriet's Underground Railroad in the Sky.* New York: Crown, 1993.

Rockwell, Anne. *The Old Woman and Her Pig and 10 Other Stories.* New York: Thomas Y. Crowell, 1979.

———. *Puss in Boots and Other Stories.* New York: Macmillan, 1988.

———. *The Three Bears & 15 Other Stories.* New York: Thomas Y. Crowell, 1975.

Rogasky, Barbara. *The Water of Life.* Illustrated by Trina Schart Hyman. New York: Holiday House, 1986.

Sendak, Maurice. *Where the Wild Things Are.* New York: Harper & Row, 1963.

Van Allsburg, Chris. *The Widow's Broom.* New York: Houghton Mifflin, 1992.

Willard, Nancy. *Beauty and the Beast.* Illustrated by Barry Moser. New York: Harcourt Brace Jovanovich, 1992.

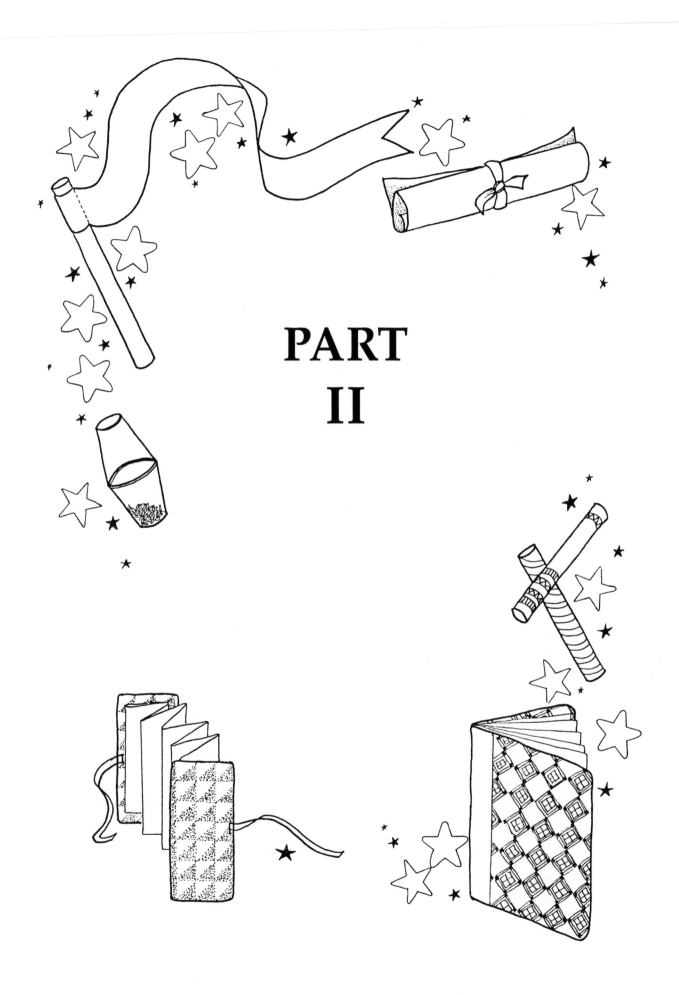

PART II

Create Your Own Instruments

As mentioned in the introduction, there are a variety of sounds that can be used for musical activities. Throughout this book, suggested musical sounds have included body and vocal sounds, found sounds, classroom instruments, traditional orchestra instruments, and homemade instruments. In the introduction are listed the instruments to use for most of the activities. Suppliers of instruments are listed in appendix D.

Some teachers, however, may want students to make their own musical instruments. The process of making instruments offers students opportunities to use various manipulative skills and follow directions. Students also can use creative processes in decorating and finding materials and abstract thinking skills ("If I add more rice in my shaker, it's going to make a louder sound," or "If I want the sound to be lower, the bar has to be longer") that sharpen musical sensitivity.

Some of the simple instruments can be made by very young students. Others are more complex and require carpenter's tools. Obviously, if saws, hammers, and nails are being used, there must be proper instruction and supervision.

Many books with instructions for making instruments are available. Check local libraries for books listed in appendix B. Also, a public or school librarian should be able to suggest others. When you read the directions, do not become discouraged. If it looks too hard, simplify! As with any good lesson plan, recipe, or story, you may adapt it to fit what you want.

These books also will offer suggestions for using the instruments in musical activities beyond those presented in this book.

Musical Streamers

Type: Music motivator.

Materials: Plastic or wooden dowels; strips of silky fabric, ribbons, or crepe paper; tape.

Ages: 5 and up.

Teachers may want to make these instruments for very young students. By age six, students can pick out a dowel and fabric and, with a little help, can tape the fabric on the dowel. This is an excellent tool for creative movement with young students.

1. Attach a long strip of lightweight fabric or crepe paper to a dowel. Plastic dowels are safer, especially with younger students. At fabric stores or recycling stores, one can usually find quantities of inexpensive fabric. Experiment with different kinds of fabric, avoiding heavier ones.

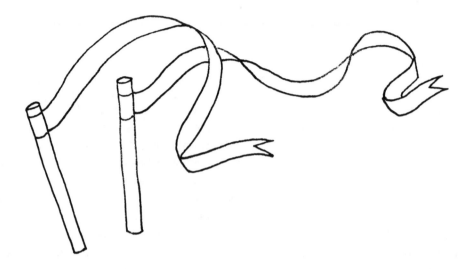

2. Tape record some short samples of music such as those in the musical activity "Changing Times" (chapter 1). Have the class wave their streamers according to how they interpret the music.

3. Play a piece of music and keep the beat to the music. Play "Follow the Leader" and change the pattern. Class follows, waving streamers.

4. Have the class move streamers according to the general feeling of the music. Stop the music at unexpected times. Students stop waving streamers when the music stops.

Shaker Cups

Type: Percussion instrument.

Materials: A variety of containers (yogurt cups, pudding cups, plastic or plastic foam cups, etc.); a variety of fillings: different kinds of dried beans (lentil, kidney, pea, etc.), rice, unpopped popcorn; masking tape (preferably colored); markers; stickers.

Ages: 5 and up.

The maraca is the most popular percussion instrument that is shaken. Maracas are typically found throughout Latin America but also are found in other parts of the world under a variety of names. They are traditionally made with a gourd or calabash shell and dried seeds.

1. Each student uses two cups identical in size. Students fill one with a handful of the desired filling. Point out that the more filling in a shaker, the denser and louder the sound. Also point out how the size of the bean or type of filling helps determine the timbre of the sound.

2. Have students place the empty cup on top of the cup with the filling, open ends together, and tape the two together.

3. If using colored masking tape, students can decorate with strips of tape. Otherwise, they can use markers or stickers.

4. Shaker cups sound best played really fast for a surprise effect. They can also mark a simple, steady beat.

5. Students can make several shakers, adjusting the amount of filling in each cup to create a different sound. Have each student create their own rhythm pattern. Ask them to listen for the different patterns and sounds when they are played together.

6. Variation: A simpler but equally effective instrument can be made with a one-piece box, such as a computer disk box. Simply fill with desired filling and tape shut. Band-Aid boxes also work well.

7. Variation: Because boxes are opaque, they are ideal for playing sound games, even with young students.

   a. Fill several containers with different materials. Have students categorize according to volume of sound (softest, medium, loudest).

   b. Fill several camera film containers with a variety of materials. Make a sound board with a sample of each filling on the board and label A, B, C, and so on. Some filling suggestions include cotton balls, unpopped popcorn, paper clips, buttons, marbles, and pebbles. Students shake the containers and indicate what they think is in each container by placing it on a sample on the sound board.

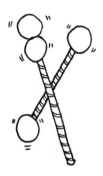

8. Variation: Make a pair of maracas by using two chopsticks and four Ping-Pong balls. Punch two holes in each ball, on opposite ends, so that the ball fits securely on the chopstick. Push a chopstick through the first hole of a ball. Before pushing the chopstick out through the second hole, carefully fill the ball with a little rice or popcorn. Place two balls on each chopstick. Shake away!

Rhythm Sticks

Type: Percussion instrument.

Materials: Wooden dowels, 1/2 to 1 inch in diameter; colored masking tape.

Ages: 6 and up.

Even students up through junior high school enjoy using rhythm sticks. Activities and games using rhythm sticks can be simple or highly complex.

1. Have students wrap each stick with a long piece of colored masking tape to resemble a candy cane or barber pole, or they may wrap any way they wish.

2. Follow the leader: Play a four-beat pattern, and the class follows.

3. Use any of the High/Scope recordings to create rhythmic patterns to accompany the music (see appendix C).

4. Have students compose rhythm patterns and create musical compositions of their own. (See chapter 3 for composition ideas.)

5. Have students create patterns of sound and silence.

6. For older students, play mixed meter games such as "Two's and Three's." Students sit in a circle, each with a pair of rhythm sticks. Students follow this pattern of three/three/two beats:

> *First measure*—Tap sticks on floor (first beat); tap sticks together (second beat); tap sticks together (third beat).
>
> *Second measure*—Repeat first measure.
>
> *Third measure*—Tap sticks on floor (first beat); pass to person on the left (second beat).
>
> Repeat entire sequence.

The idea is to keep the steady rhythmic pattern with shifting accent, without changing the speed. The notation looks like this:

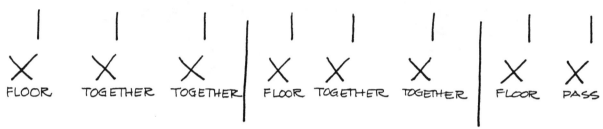

Guiro

Type: Percussion instrument.

Materials: Corrugated cardboard, plastic container lid, yarn, scissors, stapler, paper punch.

Ages: 6 and up.

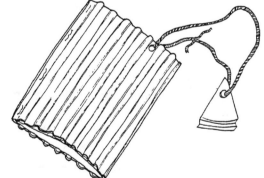

A guiro (pronounced "we-row") is a South American percussion instrument that resembles a fish. The outside has ridges that are scraped with a stick to make a grinding sound. The guiro is best used as an accompaniment to singing, instrumental pieces, and games, or as a source for sound stories.

1. Cut a piece of corrugated cardboard about 12 inches by 6 inches. Fold in half and staple together along the end opposite the fold. The hand is inserted in one of the open edges.

2. To play the guiro, students scrape the cardboard with a pencil or a pick (similar to a guitar pick). To make a simple pick, cut a triangle from a plastic container top. Punch a hole in the plastic triangle to thread yarn through and attach to the guiro by punching a hole in the cardboard.

Sandpaper Blocks

Type: Percussion instrument.

Materials: Scrap pieces of wood about 4 inches by 4 inches, sandpaper (various grades), glue.

Ages: 6 and up.

Sandpaper blocks are easy to make and add an interesting timbre and texture to music.

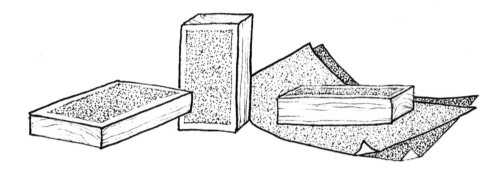

1. Have students glue pieces of sandpaper on one side of each block. Use the same grade sandpaper for each pair of blocks.

2. Allow students to rub the blocks together to create interesting sounds.

3. Experiment with various grades for various colors. A finer textured sandpaper creates a softer sound; coarser sandpaper makes louder sounds.

4. Here is a sound story to use with three different sets of sandpaper blocks. The softest ones use a very fine grade of sandpaper, the medium sound is created by a coarser grade, and the loudest sound is made by a very coarse grade. This story works best in a learning station in the classroom. Tape the following story, leaving pauses for students to say their names and play the appropriate sandblock. Make placemats for the blocks that say "Far Away," "Closer/Leaving the Station," and "At the Station," so students can place the correct blocks on the appropriate placemat. This exercise helps students sharpen their listening skills. Be creative! Make more sound stories.

The Train Ride

(name) _____was excited because today (name)_____ was going on a train ride! (name) _____went down to the station to wait for the train, which was coming from (city)_____.
As (name) _____ waited at the depot, they heard a sound that sounded "Far Away" [pause for sound]. It must still be "Far Away" [pause for sound] because (name) _____ could hardly hear it. But now it must be getting "Closer" [pause for sound]. The train tracks curved so (name) _____ couldn't see the train yet. But (name) _____ could hear it coming "Closer" [pause for sound]. It was definitely the train! Suddenly, the sound was deafening. It was "At the Station" [pause for sound]. It was here! Everybody got on the train, including (name) _____. People on the platform waved at everybody on the train. Then the train "At the Station" [pause for sound] started again. It was still loud! As the train was "Leaving the Station" [pause for sound] it began to move faster and faster. It passed the bend. After a period of time, the people on the platform could hear only the train moving "Far Away" [pause for sound]. The train was on its way to (destination)_____.

Instruments from Junk

Type: Any type of instrument.

Materials: Assorted objects of wood, glass, metal, plastic.

Ages: 9 and up.

We have found this successful for older students. It is great for creative thinking. See the introduction and chapter 2 for discussions of found sounds. This is really an extension of found sounds.

1. Place various objects in a big box. Also have available string, scissors, tape, staples, hammers, and so on, for putting together instruments. The following are some possible objects to put in the box:

    buttons (various sizes)

    nails (various sizes)

    glass bottles, jars, plastic milk jugs

    metal pans, pie plates, and so on

    paint brushes

    coffee cans

    spoons

    various kitchen tools (egg slicer, whisk, egg beater, margarine containers, spatulas, etc.)

2. Give students time to create their instruments.

3. Variation: Gather things from a specific place: outside, bathroom, kitchen, kids' room. Divide the class into groups and give each group the things from one place. Or students themselves can choose a place and the sounds. They are to make instruments from these things. Groups should not let each other see what they have.

4. After they have their instruments and sounds constructed, students create a simple musical composition, sound story, or rhythmic line. They perform this behind a screen or with their backs to the rest of the class. The class must determine which place the sounds come from.

Panpipes

Type: Wind instrument.

Materials: Plastic PVC tubing about 1/2 inch in diameter (available by the yard at hardware stores); sharp knife, razor, or tube cutter; non-hardening clay; foam core; permanent markers; masking tape.

Ages: 10 and up.

One of the oldest and simplest flutes, panpipes are still played in various parts of the world.

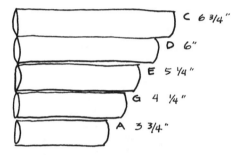

1. Using a sharp knife or razor, cut tubing into desired lengths. The teacher should cut the PVC tubing because that part can be dangerous for students. To achieve correct pitches, use the following pipe lengths: C = 6-3/4 inches; D = 6 inches; E = 5-1/4 inches; A = 3-3/4 inches; G = 4-1/4 inches.

    Any number of tubes can be used in a set of panpipes. Traditional panpipes have pentatonic tuning (five tones: C, D, E, G, and A).

2. The rest of the process can be done by students: Insert a piece of clay in the bottom of each tube. The pitch of each tube can be altered by putting more clay in the bottom. The more clay, the higher the sound. Also, be sure the bottom is completely plugged, or the tube will not sound.

3. Arrange the tubes side by side in decreasing lengths, keeping the top edges level. Wrap a piece of masking tape around to hold together.

4. Cut two pieces of foam core the size of the panpipes and attach to the instrument with masking tape.

5. Decorate the foam core with markers. To play the panpipes, blow across the top of each pipe, as if blowing across the top of a soda bottle.

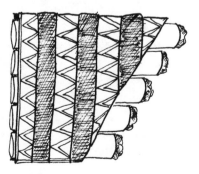

Xylophone

Type: Percussion Instrument.

Materials: Strips of hardwood such as oak, 1 inch wide by 1/4 inch thick; scraps of wood for base, 1-1/4 inches wide by 1/2 inch thick; foam insulator tape, 1/4 inch wide; nails; glue; hammer; drill; hacksaw.

Ages: 11 and up.

A xylophone is a set of wooden bars of different lengths that are played with mallets. They produce a crisp, clear, sound that is good for playing rhythms and melodies. This xylophone pattern is fairly simple. The difficulty lies in tuning the instrument. As with panpipes, the bars can be made shorter, but it is impossible to lengthen them. A pitch pipe or tuned instrument should be available to tune the bars. The teacher should cut the base pieces to size for students.

1. Cut 1-inch-wide strips of hardwood for the bars. A 10-inch-long strip should produce the note "C." Each succeeding bar should be about 3/4 inches shorter than the one before to produce a C major scale. Cut eight bars for the C scale. Gently sand down the edges so there are no slivers of wood; however, too much sanding can change the pitch. Again, these lengths are approximate. The best way to tune the bar is to keep striking it while cutting it, until the desired pitch is reached.

2. To make the base: using the wood that is 1-1/4 wide, saw off four lengths from: two about 12 inches long, one about 5 inches long (half as long as your longest bar), and the last about half that length—about 2-1/2 inches.

3. Glue the shorter lengths under the longer ones with the long lengths narrowing in, as shown in the figure on page 133.

4. Glue a strip of foam insulating tape on the top of each of the long base pieces. The bars rest on the tape.

5. Gently nail each bar through the tape and into the base. Start each hole first with the drill. The bars should be free from the base and not tightly nailed down. When struck in the middle, the bars should resonate freely. If not, they are too tight and should be loosened.

6. Nail in order of the scale, with the longest bar on the wide end and shortest bar at the narrow end.

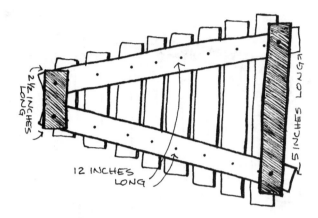

7. Tuning: This can be tricky. If a bar sounds too low, saw off a tiny bit at one end. If the sound is too high, lower the note slightly by making a saw-cut in the underpart of the bar, near each edge. You can make bigger or smaller xylophones by varying the size of the base and bars. The kind of wood used will also determine the timbre of the instrument. Any hardwood will work, but do not use plywood or pressed wood for the bars.

8. A simple pair of mallets can be made by using a length of dowel and an end piece for each mallet. End pieces can be made by attaching another short piece of dowel crosswise. Drill a hole in the end piece to insert the longer length of dowel. Or, a hard rubber super ball or a large bead can be stuck on the end of a dowel.

Tubular Bells

Type: Percussion instrument.

Materials: Copper tubing, about 3/4 inches wide; heavy dowels; heavy string; hacksaw or pipe cutter; drill.

Ages: 11 and up.

Tubular bells can create the sound of church bells. The longer the bell, the more dramatic the sound. Smaller ones can evoke the sound of chimes, especially when lightly struck. Tubular bells, like the xylophone, are pitched. However, even if they are slightly out of tune, interesting chimes can be achieved using these bells. They will add color to any musical activity. The teacher should saw and drill the pipes for younger students.

1. Saw off an 11-inch piece of tubing, which should give a "C." Tune it to another source. If it is low, trim a bit off. Cut seven more tubes, each shorter by about an inch, to give an octave.

2. Drill a tiny hole on either side of the top of each tube. Thread the string through the holes and tie to the dowel as shown. Balance the dowel between two chairs.

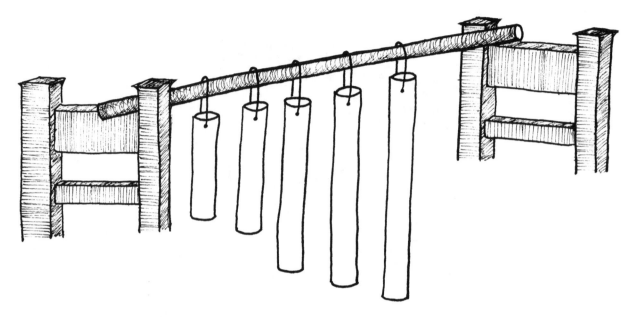

3. The xylophone mallets can be used for the tubular bells.

Appalachian Dulcimer

Type: String instrument.

Materials: Dulcimer kit from Backyard Music, paint, phillips screwdriver, glue, sandpaper, wood stain, hammer.

Ages: 10 and up.

The Appalachian dulcimer is a truly American instrument, born out of the coal mining years of the 1800s. Though reminiscent of instruments from Europe that were familiar to coal miners—the zither and the scheitholt—the dulcimer has a character of its own. Played by strumming with a pick, the dulcimer is a lap instrument. It is traditionally played by droning the lower two strings and playing the melody on the upper string, using a finger or a noter to create the pitch. The strings are traditionally tuned a fifth apart, the lowest string a fifth lower than the upper two strings, which are tuned in unison.

We recommend the Backyard Music kit, which costs about $45 and is well worth it. Dulcimers made from these kits are very durable—we have used the same one for years. The instructions are easy to follow. All the parts, including the strings, come with the kit. The body of the instrument is made of corrugated cardboard, which is folded into the body shape. The fret board is made of wood and comes pre-fretted. Each kit includes an instruction and song book.

When making the instruments, it is best to work in pairs, because some steps require two people. The fun part is decorating. Let students add their artistic inspirations to their instruments. In appendix D is a list of books and recording artists for the Appalachian dulcimer, as well as the address for Backyard Music.

Bullroarer

Type: Wind instrument.

Materials: Block of wood about 6 inches by 1 inch by 1/4 inch thick; heavy string, yarn, or nylon thread; paint and brushes for decorating; saw; drill.

Ages: 7 and up.

Although students as young as seven can play the bullroarer, have an adult saw the wood blocks and drill the holes in the top.

Caution: These instruments can be dangerous. Use under supervision. Make sure that the players have adequate space around them for the whirling instruments.

This is by far the coolest instrument we have ever made. The way it creates sounds and the sounds themselves are incredible. As stated above, the bullroarer requires a lot of space to create its sound. It is a Native American instrument, used for ritual and ceremonial purposes.

1. Saw pieces of wood to the dimensions given above. Drill a hole in one of the short sides about 1/2 inch from the top.

2. Thread a long piece (approximately 4 feet) of string, yarn, or nylon thread through the wood piece. Knot the ends.

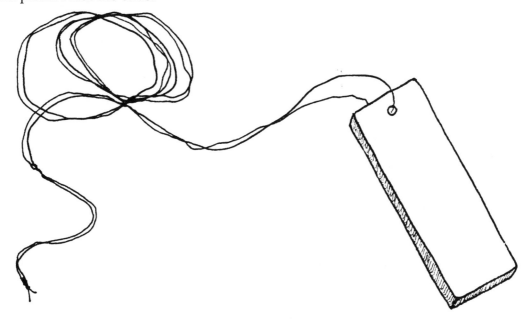

3. Have students paint any way they wish.

4. To use, students whirl the instrument around and around in big vertical circles in front of them. As the instrument goes faster, it creates a roar. Students may experiment with twirling the instrument above their heads and at different speeds to create different timbres and volume. Again, caution users to be aware of those around them. It is best to play with this instrument as Native Americans do—*outside!*

6 Bookmaking

Transcribing stories into books is an affirmation of imagination's power and permanence. Students' well-wrought stories deserve to be recorded. This chapter presents various forms of books to make in the classroom, some a little easier than others, but all well worth the time and effort.

Although students' stories may be printed from a word processor or computer and bound or pasted into a handmade book's pages, the following book formats are primarily intended for handwritten transcripts, with illustrations as desired, in the venerable tradition of illuminated manuscripts. From the earliest attempts to collect words between covers, a wide variety of materials have been tried: tablets of stone, wood, lead, bronze, and brass; strips of leather and linen; animal bones; bricks; shells; ivory; bark; even leaves of trees, before parchment and paper became the preferred mediums. Writing instruments have included various types of styluses, chisels, awls, thorns, knives, brushes for painting with colored inks, as well as the pens, pencils, and markers familiar to us. Including a brief history of these materials and of bookmaking will give context and importance to your students' own handmade books. (See appendix B, "Books About Music, Making Instruments, and Making Books.")

The most important material to have on hand for these projects is paper, from construction paper to beautifully designed wrapping papers. Each book design below specifies one or more types of appropriate paper, but here are some general guidelines for paper choices and the simplest ways to shape paper into a basic book for ages 5-9.

1. The easiest papers to use are construction and typing papers, folded in half and stapled along the fold, or two-hole punched and tied with string, ribbon, or a shoelace. The cover and pages should be gently creased next to the staples or tie so they may be turned without tearing.

2. Particularly good for primary students is unused computer paper. Its larger page size and folded format are perfect for young fingers with fat crayons. Tear off a few pages and fold along the scores for the simplest book.

3. Another simple book format is the scroll: no cover, no signatures, just a 2-to-4-foot length of paper rolled and tied. Plain shelf paper, whole or cut in half lengthwise, works well.

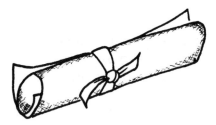

4. When selecting cover and end papers, look for elegant designs and colors. Fine wrapping paper, often available in museum shops, is excellent. Try to coordinate cover and end papers. Oriental designs and rice papers are particularly appropriate for the small Japanese folding books. These miniature books use so little cover paper that one or two sheets of wrapping paper will be enough for a whole class, so indulge in the best you can find. Students will appreciate the look and feel of quality paper.

5. The story itself may, of course, be written with pen or pencil. Consider also colored pencils, some of the wide variety of markers available, or a combination of these. A word here and there in bright blue or green in a line of black ink is not only emphatic but also aesthetically appealing.

   Markers are so permanent on paper that a slip of the pen or a word that somehow becomes a blot might be thought a disaster. Encourage the student to turn the blot into an asset: Change it to a flower, star, bird—any design appropriate to the context—perhaps using a smaller-nibbed pen.

6. All of the following measurements for books may be adjusted to another desired size. Measurements for pages/covers are relational to each other. Directions in each case are for one book, so that amount of materials will need to be adjusted for a class project.

Reminder: Have students complete all text transcribing on book pages *before* binding or adding the covers. Thus, they may change or add material or start over without having to remake covers.

Traditional Book

Materials: *Cover:* cover paper, 12 by 14 inches; two pieces medium-weight cardboard, 6 by 10 inches each; *signature:* one or two sheets endpaper, 12 by 9 inches each; *pages:* five or six sheets lightweight paper, 12 by 9 inches each. Needle and heavy-weight thread, scissors, rubber cement, bookbinding tape (see below).

Ages: 10 and up.

Finished size: 6 by 10 inches (closed).

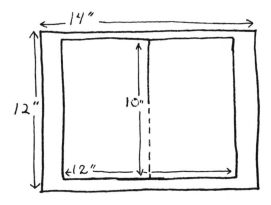

1. Cover: Spread rubber cement on the "wrong" side (inside) of the cover paper and on one side of each cardboard piece. Let dry until tacky. Place cardboard pieces on the inside of the cover paper, leaving 1/8 inch between cardboards and paper margins on all sides.

Press firmly to seal. Miter corners, leaving a small bit of cover paper to fold in toward the center of the book.

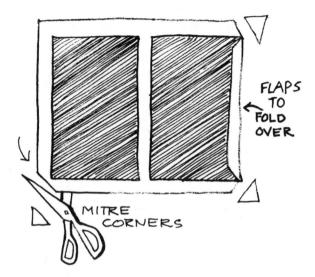

Spread rubber cement on the paper margins. When tacky, fold in all margins and press firmly to seal. From the inside, the cover now looks like the figure below.

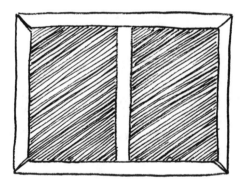

2. Signature: Fold the pages in half, with end papers on the outside. Use two pieces of end paper as the outer pages if you want the inside cover and the first loose page to match, as many end papers do.

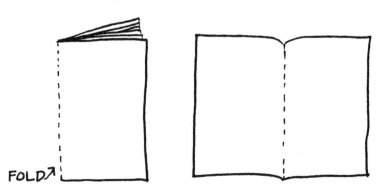

Sew the end papers and pages together with thread. Start on the outside edge of the fold with a knot. First sew up through all sheets, then sew down through all sheets; repeat this process and finish with a knot at the opposite outside edge.

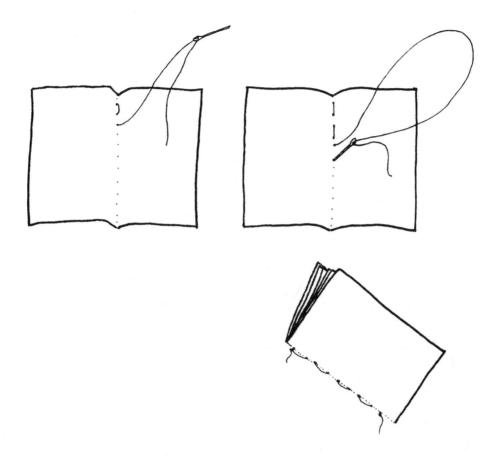

3. Assemble: Spread rubber cement on the outside-front and outside-back end papers and on the inside of both the front cover and the back cover, leaving cover margins free. Let dry until tacky. Press front and back end papers firmly in place on inside covers, with equal cover margins all around. The center fold of the signature should snuggle into the 1/8-inch center gap between the cardboards of the cover.

4. Variation: Use contact paper for cover paper, eliminating rubber cement for the cover assembly.

5. Variation: 2-inch-wide cloth (bookbinding) tape is decorative and adds a finished look to a book. Complete this step first before assembling the cover. Cut a 12-inch strip of tape and lay it flat, wrong side up. Spread rubber cement on the tape (or wet the tape if it requires moisture to stick). When the tape is tacky, place cardboard pieces on it,

leaving an 1/8-inch gap between them and a 1-inch margin of tape at the top and at the bottom. Fold these 1-inch margins of tape over the cardboard pieces to the inside.

For this variation, the cover paper is cut in two pieces, both 5-3/4 inches by 12 inches. Glue the cover paper to the cardboard as in step 1, but do the front and back separately. Cover papers should extend slightly over the tape on the outside. Assemble the cover and signature as in step 3.

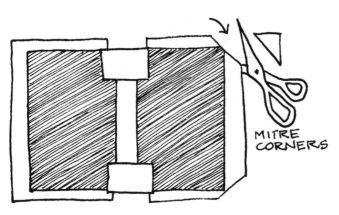

MITRE CORNERS

6. By making the back cover 1/2 inch wider at the outer edge, you may add a clever fastening for your book. Sew a 1-inch button in the center of the back cover extension, facing up. Slip the edge of the front cover under the inside of the button.

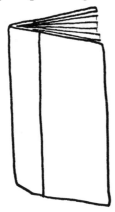

BUTTON FASTENING

Japanese Folding Book

Materials: Adding machine tape; one index card or file folder; cover paper; fine gold or silver cord, or narrow ribbon (1/16 inch); rubber cement; scissors.

Ages: 10 and up.

1. Pages: Cut a 27-inch strip of adding machine tape. Fold lengthwise in 3-inch segments, back and forth in a fan fold, keeping edges and folds absolutely even. This will give seven actual pages, with the first and last segments as bases for the covers.

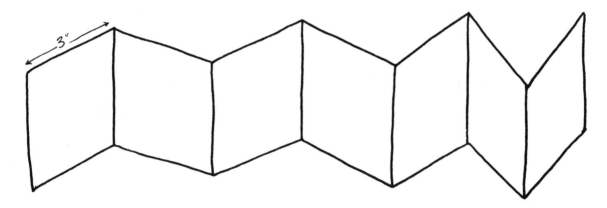

2. Covers: Cut two pieces from the index card or file folder, each two and one quarter by three inches. Glue one card to each end page as a cover base. Cut four pieces of cover paper, each 2-1/4 by 3 inches. Glue two of these pieces over the inside and outside of the front cover. If desired, cut one of these pieces slightly larger and fold it to the inside for a smooth edge.

   Before finishing the back cover in the same manner, glue ribbon or cord to the cardboard, centered, with equal lengths extending on both sides.

3. Glue cover paper on both sides of back cover, covering the ribbon. The ribbon or cord is tied around the folded book, either one way or two ways, depending on length, to make a charming package (see p. 144).

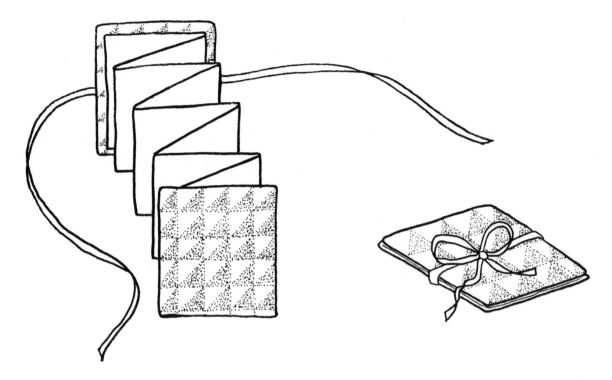

4. Variation: After the book is completely assembled, the edges may be cut into interesting shapes, either the pages alone, or pages and covers together. For example, the corners can be rounded, or V-shapes or curves can be cut at top and bottom. Be careful not to cut into the folds too much or the book will fall apart. The pages may be trimmed with pinking shears before assembling for an interesting effect.

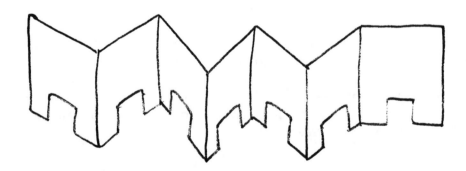

5. Variation: This is actually a two-sided book, ten pages in all, suggesting creative possibilities. The format of this variation allows students to experiment with story layout. They may wish to add more pages to their folding books for this variation. Simply cut a longer strip of adding machine tape, and fold as above. Cut windows of

various shapes in several pages, even in alternate pages (so that what is written or pictured on one side can show through).

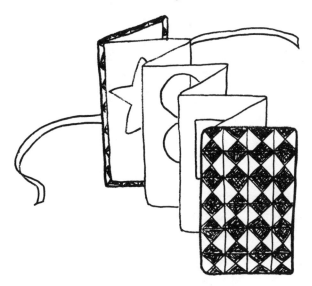

Write some words or sentences around these windows, or through the cutouts onto the other side. Or, the story may be told all on one side, with illustrations on the other.

The Unfolding Story

Materials: Light- to medium-weight paper square, 8-1/2 by 8-1/2 inches or desired size.

Ages: 10 and up.

1. Fold each corner of the square to the center.

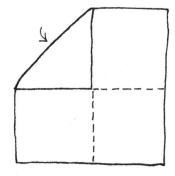

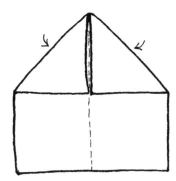

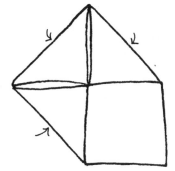

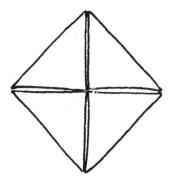

2. Fold the same way again.

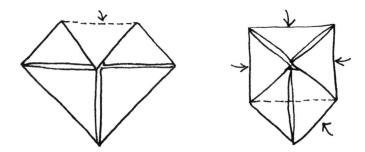

3. The story may be written from the outside in, or from the inside out. Let the crease lines and folds encourage creative placement of words and pictures. Starting from the outside, number each flap point 1, 2, 3, and 4.

Begin writing a story on flap number 1, continue on flap number 2, and so on. To continue the story after the tops of the flaps have been filled, lift flap number 1, write under that flap, then under flap number 2, and so on. Save some space for illustrations. Windows may be cut, as in the second variation for the Japanese folding book.

4. Variation: Students may experiment with other folding possibilities, other angles and shapes. For example, start with a sheet that is 8-1/2 by 11 inches. Fold one end up a third, as if for a letter. Fold the two top corners down, and let students' imaginations carry them from there.

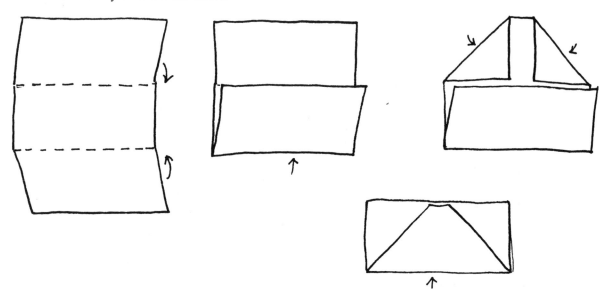

Small curls of paper or tiny figures may be attached in creative ways, to pop up as folds are opened, or to extend through windows.

POP-UP
TABS

LOOPS

PLEATS

A sentence or two of the story may be written on a strip of paper that uncurls. Miniature books or pages may be added to a folded area. Imaginative possibilities abound.

The Pocket Book

Materials: Same materials as "Traditional Book" (see p. 139); extra paper (e.g., art paper, construction paper) for pockets and figures; fabric and craft scraps.

Ages: 10 and up.

1. The basic pocket book is made exactly like the traditional book, then a "pocket" is added on the bottom half of each page by gluing a half sheet on three sides of the page. If using dark paper for the pocket, paste a piece of white or light-colored paper on the pocket front for transcribing the story, leaving a small margin on all sides. Students may wish to place pockets on alternate pages only, leaving the reverse sides of pages for the story.

2. Design and cut out several story characters or objects from paper for each pocket. Decorate with fabric scraps, cotton, yarn, buttons, and so on, for clothing, fur, or any appropriate feature. These are meant to be removable and should be compatible with each page's illustration, which is on the top half of the page, above the pocket. Illustration and characters should fit with the portion of the story on that page.

3. If desired, students may move characters from page to page as the story is retold or read.

Appendix

BOOKS ABOUT STORYTELLING/PICTURE BOOKS

Folktales in Picture-Book Format

Aardema, Verna. *Who's in Rabbit's House?* Illustrated by Leo Dillon and Diane Dillon. New York: Dial, 1977.

———. *Why Mosquitoes Buzz in People's Ears*. Illustrated by Leo Dillon and Diane Dillon. New York: Dial, 1975.

Anderson, Hans Christian. *The Nightingale*. Illustrated by Nancy Ekholm Burkert. Translated by Eva Le Gallienne. New York: Harper & Row, 1985.

———. *The Snow Queen*. Retold by Amy Ehrlich. Illustrated by Susan Jeffers. New York: Dial, 1982.

Bang, Molly. *The Paper Crane*. New York: Greenwillow, 1985.

Barton, Bob. *The Reindeer Herder and the Moon*. Illustrated by Wayne Anderson. London: BBC Educational, 1990.

———. *The Storm Wife*. Illustrated by Georgi Yudin. Kingston, Ontario: Quarry Press, 1993.

Bell, Anthea. *The Golden Moose*. New York: Henry Holt, 1988.

Brett, Jan. *Beauty and the Beast*. New York: Clarion Books, 1989.

———. *The Mitten*. New York: G. P. Putnam's Sons, 1989.

Brown, Marcia. *Once Upon a Mouse*. New York: Scribner's, 1981.

———. *Shadow*. New York: Scribner's, 1982.

———. *Stone Soup*. New York: Scribner's, 1947.

Brown, Marcia. *Cinderella*. New York: Scribner's, 1954.

Bruchac, Joseph. *The Great Ball Game: A Muskogee Story*. Illustrated by Susan L. Roth. New York: Dial, 1994.

Bruchac, Joseph, and Jonathon London. *Thirteen Moons on Turtle's Back: A Native American Year of Moons*. Illustrated by Thomas Locker. New York: Philomel Books, 1992.

Cauley, Lorinda. *Jack and the Beanstalk*. New York: G. P. Putnam's Sons, 1983.

Chief Seattle. *Brother Eagle, Sister Sky*. Illustrated by Susan Jeffers. New York: Dial, 1991.

Climo, Shirley. *The Egyptian Cinderella*. Illustrated by Ruth Heller. New York: HarperCollins, 1989.

Cooney, Barbara. *Chanticleer and the Fox.* New York: Thomas Y. Crowell, 1958.

Cooper, Susan. *The Selkie Girl.* Illustrated by Warwick Hutton. New York: Macmillan, 1986.

———. *The Silver Cow: A Welsh Tale.* Illustrated by Warwick Hutton. New York: Atheneum, 1983.

Croll, Carolyn. *The Three Brothers: A German Folktale.* New York: G. P. Putnam's Sons, 1991.

Dee, Ruby. *Two Ways to Count to Ten.* Illustrated by Susan Meddaugh. New York: Henry Holt, 1988.

dePaola, Tomie. *The Legend of Old Befana.* New York: Harcourt Brace Jovanovich, 1980.

de Regniers, Beatrice Schenk. *Jack and the Beanstalk.* Illustrated by Anne Wilsdorf. New York: Atheneum, 1985.

Domanska, Janina. *The Turnip.* New York: Macmillan, 1969.

Edens, Cooper. *Beauty and the Beast.* San Diego, Calif.: Green Tiger Press, 1989.

Esbensen, Barbara Juater. *The Star Maiden: An Ojibway Tale.* Illustrated by Helen K. Davie. Boston: Little, Brown, 1988.

Forest, Heather. *The Baker's Dozen: A Colonial American Tale.* Illustrated by Susan Gaber. New York: Harcourt Brace Jovanovich, 1988.

Galdone, Paul. *The Little Red Hen.* New York: Clarion Books, 1985.

———. *The Shoemaker and the Elves.* New York: Clarion Books, 1984.

Gerson, Mary-Joan. *Why the Sky Is Far Away.* Illustrated by Hope Meryman. New York: Harcourt Brace Jovanovich, 1974.

Goble, Paul. *Iktoni and the Boulder.* New York: Orchard/Watts, 1988.

———. *Iktoni and the Ducks.* New York: Orchard/Watts, 1990.

Goode, Diane. *Cinderella.* New York: Knopf, 1988.

Haley, Gail. *Jack and the Bean Tree.* New York: Crown, 1986.

———. *A Story! A Story!* New York: Atheneum, 1970.

Heins, Paul, trans. *Snow White.* Illustrated by Trina Schart Hyman. New York: Little, Brown, 1974.

Hieatt, Constance. *Sir Gawain and the Green Knight.* Illustrated by Walter Lorraine. New York: Thomas Y. Crowell, 1967.

Hobson, Sally. *Chicken Little.* New York: Simon & Schuster, 1994.

Hodges, Margaret. *Saint George and the Dragon.* Illustrated by Trina Schart Hyman. Boston: Little, Brown, 1984.

Hutton, Warwick. *The Nose Tree.* New York: Atheneum, 1981.

Hyman, Trina Schart. *Little Red Riding Hood.* New York: Holiday House, 1983.

Irving, Washington. *The Legend of Sleepy Hollow.* Illustrated by Robert Van Nutt. Saxonville, Mass.: Picture Book Studio, 1989.

Jarrell, Randall, trans. *The Fisherman and His Wife.* Illustrated by Margot Zemach. New York: Farrar, Straus & Giroux, 1980.

———. *Snow-White and the Seven Dwarfs.* Illustrated by Nancy Ekholm Burkert. New York: Farrar, Straus & Giroux, 1972.

Jeffers, Susan. *Hansel and Gretel.* New York: Dial, 1980.

Karlin, Barbara. *Cinderella.* Illustrated by James Marshall. Boston: Little, Brown, 1989.

Kellogg, Steven. *Jack and the Beanstalk.* New York: Morrow Junior Books, 1991.

Kimmel, Eric A. *Anansi and the Moss-Covered Rock.* Illustrated by Janet Stevens. New York: Holiday House, 1988.

Langton, Jane. *The Hedgehog Boy: A Latvian Folktale.* Illustrated by Ilse Plume. New York: Harper & Row, 1985.

Lesser, Rika. *Hansel and Gretel.* Illustrated by Paul O. Zelinsky. New York: G. P. Putnam's Sons, 1984.

Lewis, Richard. *All of You Was Singing.* Illustrated by Ed Young. New York: Atheneum, 1991.

Littledale, Freya. *The Elves and the Shoemaker.* Illustrated by Brinton Turkle. New York: Four Winds Press, [c. 1975].

Lobel, Arnold. *Ming Lo Moves the Mountain.* New York: Greenwillow, 1982.

Lofts, Pamela. *Dunbi the Owl.* San Diego, Calif.: Mad Hatter Books, Slawson Communications, 1983.

Louie, Ai-Ling. *Yeh-Shen: A Cinderella Story from China.* Illustrated by Ed Young. New York: Philomel Books, 1982.

Ludwig, Warren. *Old Noah's Elephants.* New York: G. P. Putnam's Sons, 1991.

Marshall, James. *Goldilocks and the Three Bears.* New York: Dial, 1988.

———. *Red Riding Hood.* New York: Dial, 1987.

Martin, Rafe. *The Rough-Face Girl.* Illustrated by David Shannon. New York: G. P. Putnam's Sons, 1992.

Mayer, Marianna. *Beauty and the Beast.* New York: Macmillan, 1987.

McDermott, Gerald. *Anansi the Spider.* New York: Holt, Rinehart & Winston, 1972.

———. *Arrow to the Sun.* New York: Viking Press, 1974.

———. *The Stonecutter.* New York: Viking Press, 1975.

McGovern, Ann. *Too Much Noise.* Illustrated by Simms Taback. Boston: Houghton Mifflin, 1967.

McKissack, Patricia C. *Flossie & the Fox.* Illustrated by Rachel Isadora. New York: Dial, 1986.

Mikolaycak, Charles. *Babushka.* New York: Holiday House, 1984.

Mosel, Arlene. *The Funny Little Woman.* Illustrated by Blair Lent. New York: E. P. Dutton, 1972.

———. *Tikki, Tikki, Tembo.* Illustrated by Blair Lent. New York: Scholastic, 1968.

Nielsen, Kay. *East of the Sun and West of the Moon.* Garden City, N.Y.: Doubleday, 1977.

Oughton, Jerrie. *How the Stars Fell into the Sky: A Navajo Legend.* Illustrated by Lisa Desimini. Boston: Houghton Mifflin, 1992.

Plume, Ilse. *The Bremen-Town Musicians.* New York: Harper & Row, 1980.

———. *The Shoemaker and the Elves.* San Diego: Harcourt Brace Jovanovich, 1991.

Robbins, Ruth. *Baboushka and the Three Kings.* Illustrated by Nicolas Sidjakov. New York: Parnassus Press, 1960.

Rockwell, Anne. *The Old Woman and Her Pig and 10 Other Stories.* New York: Thomas Y. Crowell, 1979.

———. *Puss in Boots and Other Stories.* New York: Macmillan, 1988.

———. *The Three Bears & 15 Other Stories.* New York: Thomas Y. Crowell, 1975.

Rogasky, Barbara. *The Water of Life.* Illustrated by Trina Schart Hyman. New York: Holiday House, 1986.

San Souci, Robert D. *The Talking Eggs*. Illustrated by Jerry Pinkney. New York: Dial, 1989.

Sawyer, Ruth. *Journey Cake, Ho!* New York: Viking Press, 1982.

Stanley, Diane. *Fortune*. New York: Morrow, 1990.

Steptoe, John. *The Story of Jumping Mouse: A Native American Legend*. New York: Mulberry Books, 1972.

Stewig, John. *The Fisherman and His Wife*. Illustrated by Margot Tomes. New York: Holiday House, 1988.

Tadjo, Véronique. *Lord of the Dance: An African retelling*. New York: J. B. Lippincott, 1988.

Troughton, Joanna. *Mouse Deer's Market*. New York: Peter Bedrick Books, 1984.

Wahl, Jan. *Tailypo!* Illustrated by Wil Clay. New York: Henry Holt, 1991.

Watts, Bernadette. *The Elves and the Shoemaker*. New York: North-South Books, 1986.

Whitney, Thomas P., trans. *Vasilisa the Beautiful*. Illustrated by Nonny Hogrogian. New York: Macmillan, 1970.

Willard, Nancy. *Beauty and the Beast*. Illustrated by Barry Moser. New York: Harcourt Brace Jovanovich, 1992.

Wolkstein, Diane. *The Magic Wings*. Illustrated by Robert Andrew Parker. New York: E. P. Dutton, 1983.

Xiong, Blia. *Nine-In-One Grr! Grr!* Adapted by Cathy Spagnoli. Illustrated by Nancy Hom. San Francisco, Calif.: Children's Book Press, 1989.

Yolen, Jane. *The Girl Who Loved the Wind*. Illustrated by Ed Young. New York: Thomas Y. Crowell, 1972.

———. *Old Dame Counterpane*. Illustrated by Ruth Tietjen Councell. New York: Philomel Books, 1994.

———. *Tam Lin*. Illustrated by Charles Mikolaycak. San Diego, Calif.: Harcourt Brace Jovanovich, 1990.

Young, Ed. *Lon Po Po: A Red-Riding Hood Story from China*. New York: Philomel Books, 1989.

Zelinsky, Paul O. *Rumplestiltskin*. New York: E. P. Dutton, 1986.

Zemach, Harve. *Duffy and the Devil*. Illustrated by Margot Zemach. New York: Farrar, Straus & Giroux, 1973.

Zemach, Margot. *The Three Wishes*. New York: Farrar, Straus & Giroux, 1986.

Authored Stories in Picture-Book Format

Ada, Alma Flor. *Dear Peter Rabbit*. Illustrated by Leslie Tryon. New York: Atheneum, 1994.

Adinolfi, JoAnn. *The Egyptian Polar Bear*. Boston: Houghton Mifflin, 1994.

Ahlberg, Janet, and Allen Ahlberg. *The Jolly Christmas Postman*. New York: Little, Brown, 1991.

———. *The Jolly Postman: Or Other People's Letters*. New York: Little, Brown, 1985.

Alexander, Lloyd. *The Fortune-Tellers*. Illustrated by Trina Schart Hyman. New York: E. P. Dutton, 1992.

Allen, Pamela. *Bertie and the Bear*. New York: Coward-McCann, 1983.

Anno, Mitsumasa. *In Shadowland*. New York: Orchard Books, 1988.

Armstrong, Jennifer. *The Whittler's Tale*. Illustrated by Valery Vasiliev. New York: Tambourine Books, 1994.

Asch, Frank. *Happy Birthday, Moon.* Englewood Cliffs, N.J.: Prentice- Hall, 1982.

Baker, Keith. *The Magic Fan*. San Diego, Calif.: Harcourt Brace Jovanovich, 1989.

———. *Who Is the Beast?* San Diego, Calif.: Harcourt Brace Jovanovich, 1990.

Barrett, Judi. *Cloudy with a Chance of Meatballs*. Illustrated by Ron Barrett. New York: Atheneum, 1978.

Bedard, Michael. *Emily*. Illustrated by Barbara Cooney. New York: Doubleday, 1992.

Briggs, Raymond. *The Snowman*. New York: Random House, 1978.

Bunting, Eve. *The Man Who Could Call Down Owls.* Illustrated by Charles Mikolaycak. New York: Macmillan, 1984.

Carle, Eric. *The Grouchy Ladybug.* New York: Thomas Y. Crowell, 1977.

———. *The Secret Birthday Message.* New York: HarperCollins, 1972.

———. *I See a Song.* New York: Thomas Y. Crowell, 1973.

———. *Papa, Please Get the Moon for Me.* Saxonville, Mass.: Picture Book Studio, 1986.

———. *The Very Busy Spider.* New York: Philomel Books, 1984.

———. *The Very Hungry Caterpillar.* New York: Philomel Books, 1981.

———. *The Very Quiet Cricket.* New York: Philomel Books, 1990.

DePaola, Tomie. *When Everyone Was Fast Asleep.* New York: Holiday House, 1976.

Fleming, Denise. *In the Small, Small Pond.* New York: Henry Holt, 1993.

———. *In the Tall, Tall Grass.* New York: Henry Holt, 1991.

Gag, Wanda. *Millions of Cats.* New York: Coward-McCann, 1928.

Greene, Carol. *The Old Ladies Who Liked Cats.* Illustrated by Loretta Krupinski. New York: Harper-Collins, 1991.

Hamanaka, Sheila. *All the Colors of the Earth.* New York: Morrow, 1994.

Hutchins, Pat. *Rosie's Walk.* New York: Macmillan, 1968.

James, Simon. *Dear Mr. Blueberry.* New York: Margaret K. McElderry Books, 1991.

Johnston, Tony. *The Quilt Story.* Illustrated by Tomie dePaola. New York: G. P. Putnam's Sons, 1985.

Latimer, Jim. *When Moose Was Young.* New York: Scribner's, 1990.

Leonni, Leo. *Matthew's Dream.* New York: Knopf, 1991.

Locker, Thomas. *The Land of Gray Wolf.* New York: Dial, 1991.

Lyon, George Ella. *Five Live Bongos.* Illustrated by Jacqueline Rogers. New York: Scholastic, 1994.

McCully, Emily Arnold. *Crossing the New Bridge.* New York: G. P. Putnam's Sons, 1994.

Melmed, Laura Krauss. *Prince Nautilus.* Illustrated by Henri Sorensen. New York: Lothrop, Lee & Shephard, 1994.

Munsch, Robert. *The Paper Bag Princess.* Illustrated by Michael Martchenko. Toronto, Canada: Annick Press, 1980.

Murphy, Jill. *Peace At Last.* New York: Dial, 1980.

Numeroff, Laura Jaffe. *If You Give a Moose a Muffin.* Illustrated by Felicia Bond. New York: Harper-Collins, 1991.

———. *If You Give a Mouse a Cookie.* Illustrated by Felicia Bond. New York: Harper & Row, 1985.

Polacco, Patricia. *Pink and Say.* New York: Philomel Books, 1994.

Ringgold, Faith. *Aunt Harriet's Underground Railroad in the Sky.* New York: Crown, 1993.

Sendak, Maurice. *Pierre.* New York: Harper & Row, 1962.

———. *Where the Wild Things Are.* New York: Harper & Row, 1963.

Shea, Pegi Dietz. *The Whispering Cloth: A Refugee Story.* Illustrated by Anita Riggio; stitched by You Yang. Honesdale, Penn.: Boyds Mills Press, 1995.

Shulevitz, Uri. *Dawn.* New York: Farrar, Straus & Giroux, 1974.

Steig, William. *Zeke Pippin.* New York: HarperCollins, 1994.

Thurber, James. *Many Moons.* New York: Harcourt Brace Jovanovich, 1943.

Tusa, Tricia. *Maebelle's Suitcase.* New York: Macmillan, 1987.

Van Allsburg, Chris. *The Polar Express.* Boston: Houghton Mifflin, 1985.

———. *The Widow's Broom.* New York: Houghton Mifflin, 1992.

Weisner, David. *Tuesday.* New York: Clarion Books, 1991.

Wood, Audrey. *King Bidgood's in the Bathtub.* San Diego, Calif.: Harcourt Brace Jovanovich, 1985.

Wright, Jill. *The Old Woman and the Willy-Nilly Man.* New York: Putnam, 1987.

Yolen, Jane. *Owl Moon.* Illustrated by John Schoenherr. New York: Scholastic, 1987.

Collections of Folktales

Aardema, Verna. *Misoso: Once Upon a Time Tales from Africa.* Westminster, Md.: Knopf, 1994.

Aesop. *Fables.* New York: Viking, 1981.

Asbjornsen, Peter Christian, and Jorgen Moe. *Norwegian Folk Tales.* New York: Viking, 1960.

Babbit, Ellen C. *Jataka Tales.* New York: Appleton-Century-Crofts, 1940.

Barchers, Suzanne I. Ed. *Wise Women: Folk and Fairy Tales from Around the World.* Englewood, Colo.: Libraries Unlimited, 1990.

Bierhorst, John. *Doctor Coyote: A Native American Aesop's Fables.* New York: Macmillan, 1987.

Botkin, B. A. *A Treasury of American Folklore.* New York: Crown, 1944.

Bruchac, Joseph. *Iroquois Stories: Heroes and Heroines, Monsters and Magic.* Freedom, Calif.: Crossing Press, 1985.

Bryan, Ashley. *Beat the Story Drum, Pum, Pum.* New York: Atheneum, 1980.

Caduto, Michael J., and Joseph Bruchac. *Keepers of the Animals: Native American Stories and Wildlife Activities for Children.* Golden, Colo.: Fulcrum, 1991.

———. *Keepers of the Earth: Native American Stories and Environmental Activities for Children.* Golden, Colo.: Fulcrum, 1988.

Carey, Bonnie. *Baba Yaga's Geese and Other Russian Stories.* Bloomington: Indiana University Press, 1973.

Carter, Angela, ed. *Sleeping Beauty & Other Favourite Fairy Tales*. Boston: Houghton Mifflin, 1991.

Chase, Richard. *Grandfather Tales*. Boston: Houghton Mifflin, 1948.

Cole, Joanna. *Best-Loved Folktales of the World*. Garden City, N.Y.: Anchor Press/Doubleday, 1983.

Colwell, Eileen. *The Magic Umbrella and Other Stories for Telling*. London: Bodley Head, 1976.

Courlander, Harold. *The Cow-Tail Switch and Other West African Stories*. New York: Holt, Rinehart & Winston, 1947.

Courlander, Harold, and Albert Kofi Prempeh. *The Hat-Shaking Dance and Other Tales from the Gold Coast*. New York: Harcourt Brace, 1957.

D'Aulaire, Ingri, and Edgar D'Aulaire. *D'Aulaire's Book of Greek Myths*. Garden City, N.Y.: Doubleday, 1962.

———. *Norse Gods and Giants*. Garden City, N.Y.: Doubleday, 1967.

DeSpain, Pleasant. *Twenty-Two Splendid Tales to Tell*. 2 vols. Little Rock, Ark.: August House, 1994.

Gaer, Joseph. *The Fables of India*. Boston: Little, Brown, 1955.

Garner, Alan. *Alan Garner's Book of British Fairy Tales*. New York: Delacorte Press, 1984.

Ginsburg, Mirra. *The Three Rolls and One Doughnut: Fables from Russia*. New York: Dial, 1970.

Hamilton, Virginia. *The Dark Way: Stories from the Spirit World*. San Diego, Calif.: Harcourt Brace Jovanovich, 1990.

———. *In the Beginning: Creation Stories from Around the World*. New York: Harcourt Brace Jovanovich, 1988.

———. *The People Could Fly: Black Folktales*. New York: Knopf, 1985.

Hayes, Joe. *Coyote and. . . .* Santa Fe, N.Mex.: Mariposa, 1982.

Jacobs, Joseph. *English Fairy Tales*. New York: Putnam, 1892.

Jagendorf, M. A., and Virginia Weng. *The Magic Boat and Other Chinese Folk Stories*. New York: Vanguard Press, 1980.

Jagendorf, Moritz. *New England Bean-Pot*. New York: Vanguard Press, 1948.

———. *The Priceless Cats and Other Italian Folk Stories*. New York: Vanguard Press, 1956.

———. *Tyll Ulenspiegel's Merry Pranks*. New York: Vanguard Press, 1938.

Lester, Julius. *How Many Spots Does a Leopard Have?* New York: Scholastic, 1989.

Mayo, Margaret. *Magical Tales from Many Lands*. New York: E. P. Dutton, 1983.

McKissack, Patricia. *The Dark-Thirty: Southern Tales of the Supernatural*. New York: Knopf, 1992.

Moore, Robin. *When the Moon Is Full: Supernatural Stories from the Old Pennsylvania Mountains*. Westminster, Md.: Knopf, 1994.

Ransome, Arthur. *Old Peter's Russian Tales*. Harmondsworth, Middlesex, England: Puffin Books, Penguin Books, 1979.

Rosen, Michael. *How the Animals Got Their Colors*. San Diego, Calif.: Harcourt Brace Jovanovich, 1992.

Schwartz, Alvin. *More Scary Stories to Tell in the Dark*. New York: J. B. Lippincott, 1984.

———. *Scary Stories to Tell in the Dark*. New York: J. B. Lippincott, 1981.

Schwartz, Howard. *Elijah's Violin & Other Jewish Fairy Tales*. New York: Harper & Row, 1985.

Sherlock, Philip M. *West Indian Folk Tales*. New York: Walck, 1966.

Smith, Jimmy Neil. *Homespun: Tales from America's Favorite Storytellers.* New York: Crown, 1988.

Spellman, John. *The Beautiful Blue Jan and Other Tales of India.* Boston: Little, Brown, 1967.

Tashjian, Virginia. *Juba This and Juba That.* New York: Little, Brown, 1969.

———. *Once There Was and Was Not: Armenian Tales.* Boston: Little, Brown, 1966.

Wolkstein, Diane. *The Magic Orange Tree and Other Haitian Folktales.* New York: Schocken Books, 1980.

Yolen, Jane. *Favorite Folktales from Around the World.* New York: Pantheon, 1986.

Zipes, Jack, trans. *The Complete Fairy Tales of the Brothers Grimm.* Illustrated by John B. Gruelle. New York: Bantam Books, 1987.

Authored Stories in Collections

Kipling, Rudyard. *Just So Stories.* New York: Crown, 1978.

Lobel, Arnold. *Mouse Tales.* New York: Harper & Row, 1972.

Roberts, Bethany. *Waiting-for-Papa Stories.* Illustrated by Sarah Stapler. New York: Harper & Row, 1990.

———. *Waiting-for-Spring Stories.* Illustrated by William Joyce. New York: Harper & Row, 1984.

Yolen, Jane. *The Girl Who Cried Flowers and Other Tales.* New York: Thomas Y. Crowell, 1974.

———. *Neptune Rising: Songs & Tales of the Undersea Folk.* New York: Philomel Books, 1982.

General Fiction

Conly, Jane Leslie. *Racso and the Rats of NIMH.* New York: Harper & Row, 1986.

———. *RT, Margaret and the Rats of NIHM.* New York: Harper & Row, 1990.

Grahame, Kenneth. *The Wind in the Willows.* New York: Scribner's, 1908.

Lindbergh, Anne. *The Hunky-Dory Diary.* New York: Harcourt Brace Jovanovich, 1986.

———. *Nick of Time.* Boston: Little, Brown, 1994.

Lowry, Lois. *The Giver.* Boston: Houghton Mifflin, 1993.

Norton, Mary. *The Borrowers.* First book in The Borrowers series. New York: Harcourt Brace Jovanovich, 1952.

O'Brien, Robert C. *Mrs. Frisby and the Rats of NIMH.* New York: Atheneum, 1971.

Pearce, Philippa. *Tom's Midnight Garden.* New York: J. B. Lippincott, 1958.

White, E. B. *Charlotte's Web.* New York: Harper & Row, 1952.

Poetry Anthologies

Carle, Eric. *Animals Animals.* New York: Philomel Books, 1989.

Hubbell, Patricia. *The Tigers Brought Pink Lemonade.* New York: Atheneum, 1988.

Koch, Kenneth, and Kate Farrell. *Talking to the Sun.* New York: Holt, Rinehart & Winston, 1985.

Larrick, Nancy. *Piper, Pipe That Song Again*. New York: Random House, 1965.

———. *Piping Down the Valleys Wild*. New York: Delacorte Press, 1968.

Locker, Thomas. *Snow Toward Evening*. New York: Dial, 1990.

Merriam, Eve. *A Sky Full of Poems*. New York: Dell, 1986.

Schenk de Regniers, Beatrice, et al. New York: Scholastic, 1988.

Schwartz, Alvin. *And the Green Grass Grew All Around*. New York: HarperCollins, 1992.

Books About Stories and Storytelling

Barton, Bob. *Tell Me Another*. Markham, Ontario: Pembroke, 1986.

Barton, Bob, and David Booth. *Stories in the Classroom*. Portsmouth, N. H.: Heinemann, 1990.

Bauer, Caroline. *Caroline Feller Bauer's New Handbook for Storytellers*. Chicago: American Library Association, 1993.

Breneman, Lucille, and Bren Breneman. *Once Upon a Time: A Storytelling Handbook*. Chicago: Nelson-Hall, 1984.

Collins, Chase. *Tell Me a Stoy: Creating Bedtime Tales Your Children Will Dream On*. Boston: Houghton Mifflin, 1992.

Colwell, Eileen. *Storytelling*. London: Bodley Head, 1980.

Hamilton, Martha, and Mitch Weiss. *Children Tell Stories*. Katonah, N.Y.: Richard C. Owen, 1990.

Livo, Norma J., ed. *Joining In: An Anthology of Participation Stories and How to Tell Them*. Cambridge, Mass.: Yellow Moon Press, 1988.

Livon, Norma J. and Sandra A. Rietz. *Storytelling: Process and Practice*. Littleton, Colo.: Libraries Unlimited, 1988.

———. *Storytelling Activities*. Littleton, Colo.: Libraries Unlimited, 1987.

Maguire, Jack. *Creative Storytelling*. New York: McGraw-Hill, 1985.

Pellowski, Anne. *The Family Storytelling Handbook*. New York: Macmillan, 1987.

———. *Hidden Stories in Plants*. New York: Macmillan, 1990.

———. *The Story Vine*. New York: Collier Macmillan, 1984.

———. *The World of Storytelling*. New York: R. R. Bowker, 1977.

Sawyer, Ruth. *The Way of the Storyteller*. New York: Viking Press, 1942.

Schimmel, Nancy. *Just Enough to Make a Story*, 2d ed. Berkeley, Calif.: Sisters Choice Press, 1982.

Shedlock, Marie L. *The Art of the Storyteller*. New York: Dover, 1951.

Trelease, Jim, Ed. *Hey! Listen to This: Stories to Read Aloud*. New York: Viking Penguin, 1992.

———. *The New Read-Aloud Handbook*, 2d ed. New York: Penguin Books, 1989.

Weaver, Mary, ed. *Tales As Tools*. Jonesborough, Tenn.: National Storytelling Association Press, 1994.

Yolen, Jane. *Touch Magic: Fantasy, Faerie and Folklore in the Literature of Childhood*. New York: Philomel Books, 1981.

Appendix

BOOKS ABOUT MUSIC, MAKING INSTRUMENTS, AND MAKING BOOKS

Music History and Appreciation

De Souza, Chris. *Looking at Music*. New York: Van Nostrand Reinhold, 1979.

Foster, Karen. *Rattles, Bells, and Chiming Bars*. Brookfield, Conn.: Millbrook Press, 1990.

Hart, Mickey, and Frederic Lieberman. *Planet Drum—A Celebration of Percussion and Rhythm*. New York: HarperCollins, 1991.

Hurd, Michael. *The Orchestra*. New York: Facts on File, 1980.

Machlis, Joseph. *The Enjoyment of Music*. New York: W. W. Norton, 1977.

Menuhin, Yehudi, and Curtis W. Davis. *The Music of Man*. Toronto: Methuen, 1979. Parker, Josephine. *Music from Strings*. Brookfield, Conn.: Millbrook Press, Merion, 1992.

Sommer, Elyse. *The Kids World Almanac of Music*. New York: World Almanac Pharos Books, 1991.

Staples, Danny, and Carole Mahoney. *Flutes, Reeds, and Trumpets*. Brookfield, Conn.: Millbrook Press, 1992.

Weil, Lisl. *The Magic of Music*. New York: Holiday House, 1989.

Music Education and Theory

Campbell, Don G. *Introduction to the Musical Brain*. St. Louis, Mo.: MMB Music, 1983.

Children as Music Makers. The Cognitively Oriented Curriculum. Ypsilanti, Mich.: High/Scope Educational Research, 1979.

Hart, Avery, and Paul Mantell. *Kids Make Music*. Charlotte, Vt.: Williamson, 1993.

Kaplan, Don G. *See With Your Ears—The Creative Music Book*. San Francisco, Calif.: Lexikos, 1983.

Mathieu, W. A. *The Listening Book—Discovering Your Own Music*. Boston: Shambhala, 1991.

Schafer, R. Murray. *Creative Music Education*. New York: Schirmer Books, 1976.

Spanko, Jean. *Taming the Anthill*. Memphis, Tenn.: MMP, 1985.

Weikert, Phyllis. *Teaching Movement and Dance.* Ypsilanti, Mich.: High/Scope Press, 1982.

Wood, Donna. *Move, Sing, Listen, Play—Preparing the Young Child for Music.* Toronto: Gordon V. Thompson, 1982.

Sound Experiments and Exploration

Ardley, Neil. *Hands on Science: Sound Waves to Music.* New York: Gloucester Press, 1990.

Broekel, Ray. *Sound Experiments.* Chicago: Children's Press, 1988.

Darlin, David. *Sounds Interesting. The Science of Acoustics.* New York: Macmillan, 1991.

Davies, Kay, and Wendy Oldfield. *Starting Science: Sound and Music.* Austin, Tex.: Steck-Vaughn Library, 1992.

Ward, Alan. *Project Science: Sound and Music.* New York: Franklin Watts, 1992.

Instrument Making

Banek, Reinhold, and Jon Scoville. *Sound Designs: A Handbook of Music Instrument Building.* Berkeley, Calif.: Ten Speed Press, 1980.

Botemans, Jack, and Herman Dewit. *Making and Playing Musical Instruments.* Seattle: University of Washington Press, 1989.

Bristol, Marc. *Homegrown Music.* Seattle, Wash.: Madrona, 1982.

Collier, James Lincoln. *Jug Bands and Handmade Music.* New York: Grosset & Dunlap, 1973.

Drew, Helen. *My First Music Book.* New York: Dorling Kindersley, 1993.

Garnett, Hugh. *Musical Instruments You Can Make.* London: Pitman, 1976.

Hunter, Ilene, and Marilyn Judson. *Simple Folk Instruments to Make and to Play.* New York: Simon & Schuster, 1977.

Magadini, Peter. *Music We Can See and Hear.* Oakville, Ontario: Frederick Harris Music, 1982.

Mandell, Muriel, and Robert E. Wood. *Make Your Own Musical Instruments.* New York: Sterling, 1957.

McLean, Margaret. *Make Your Own Musical Instruments.* Minneapolis, Minn.: Lerner, 1988.

Sloane, Irving. *Making Musical Instruments.* New York: E. P. Dutton, 1978.

Turner, Barrie Carson. *I Like Music.* New York: Warwick Press, 1989.

Waring, Dennis. *Making Folk Instruments in Wood.* New York: Sterling, 1979.

Song Books

East, Helen, comp. *The Singing Sack 28 Song-Stories from Around the World.* London: A & C Black, 1989.

Fox, Dan, and Claude Marks. *Go In and Out the Window. Illustrated Songbook for Young People.* New York: Metropolitan Museum of Art, Henry Holt, 1987.

Hart, Jane. *Singing Bee.* New York: Lothrop, Lee & Shepherd, 1982.

Langstaff, John. *Hot Cross Buns and Other Old Street Cries.* New York: Atheneum, 1978.

Seeger, Ruth Crawford. *American Folk Songs for Children*. Garden City, N.Y.: Doubleday, 1948.

Sharon, Lois, and Bram Sharon. *Elephant Jam*. Toronto: McGraw-Hill Ryerson, 1980.

———. *Mother Goose*. New York: Atlantic Monthly Press, 1985.

Simon, William W., ed. *The Reader's Digest Children's Songbook*. Pleasantville, N.Y.: Reader's Digest, 1985.

Wirth, Marian, et al. *Musical Games, Fingerplays and Rhythmic Activities for Early Childhood*. West Nyack, N.Y.: Parker, 1981.

Withers, Carl, comp. *A Rocket in my Pocket the Rhymes and Chants of Young Americans*. New York: Scholastic Press, 1948.

Picture Books About Music

Ackerman, Karen. *Song and Dance Man*. Illustrated by Stephen Gammell. New York: Knopf, 1988.

Baer, Gene. *Thump, Thump, Rat-a-Tat-Tat*. Illustrated by Lois Ehlert. New York: HarperCollins, 1989.

Brett, Jan. *Berlioz the Bear*. New York: G. P. Putnam's Sons , 1991.

Fleischman, Paul. *Rondo in C*. Illustrated by Janet Wentworth. New York: Harper & Row, 1988.

Komaiko, Leah. *I Like the Music*. Illustrated by Barbara Westman. New York: Harper & Row, 1987.

Lyon, George Ella. *Five Live Bongos*. Illustrated by Jacqueline Rogers. New York: Scholastic, 1994.

Martin, Bill, Jr., and John Archambault. *Barn Dance*. Illustrated by Ted Rand. New York: Henry Holt, 1986.

Sage, James. *The Little Band*. Illustrated by Keiko Narahashi. New York: Macmillan, 1991.

Seeger, Pete. *Abiyoyo*. Illustrated by Michael Hays. New York: Macmillan, 1985.

Spier, Peter. *The Erie Canal*. New York: Doubleday, 1970.

Walter, Mildred Pitts. *Ty's One-Man Band*. Illustrated by Margot Tomes. New York: Four Winds Press, 1980.

Williams, Vera B. *Music, Music for Everyone*. New York: Greenwillow, 1984.

Zemach, Margot. *All God's Critters Got a Place in the Choir*. New York: E. P. Dutton, 1989.

Bookmaking

Chapman, Gillian, and Pam Robson. *Making Books: A Step-by-Step Guide to Your Own Publishing*. Brookfield, Conn.: Millbrook Press, 1992.

Donaldson, Gerald. *Books*. New York: Van Nostrand Reinhold, 1987.

Feather, John. *A Dictionary of Book History*. New York: Oxford University Press, 1986.

Greenfield, Howard. *Books from Writer to Reader*. New York: Crown, 1989.

McClymont, Diane. *Books*. Ada, Okla.: Garrett, 1991.

Olmert, Michael. *The Smithsonian Book of Books*. Washington, D.C.: Smithsonian Press, 1992.

Suhr, Mandy. *Making a Book*. New York: Thomson Learning, 1993.

Vervliet, H. D. L., ed. *The Book Through 5000 Years*. London: Phaidon Press, 1972.

Appendix

RECORDING REFERENCES

Bach, Johann Sebastian. "Air on a G String," from *Bach's Greatest Hits*. RCA 60828-2-RG (CD); 60828-4-RG6 (cassette).

———. *Brandenburg Concerto no. 2 BWV 1047*. Marlboro Festival Orchestra. Casals. CBS MLK-39442 (CD); MT-39442 (cassette).

———. "Jesu, Joy of Man's Desiring," from *Bach's Greatest Hits*. RCA 60828-2-RG (CD); 60828-4-RG6 (cassette).

———. "Prelude," from *Partita for Solo Violin BWV 1001*. Milstein. Deutsche Grammophone CD-423294-2 GCM2 (CD).

———. "Prelude," from *Partita for Solo Violin BWV 1001*. Heifetz. RCA Gold Seal 7708-2 RG (CD); 7708-4 RRG 13 (cassette).

———. *Two Part Inventions BWV 772-786*. Malcolm, Harpsichord. Elektra/Nonesuch 71144-4 (cassette).

———. *Two Part Inventions BWV 772-786*. Schiff, Piano. London 411974-2 LH (CD).

Ball, Patrick. *The Ugly Duckling*. Windham Hill/Rabbit Ears Storybook Classics WD-0705 (CD); WT-0705 (cassette).

Barber, Samuel. "Adagio for Strings" from *Romantic Favorites for Strings*. New York Philharmonic Orchestra. Bernstein. CBS MYK-38484 (CD); MYT-38484 (cassette).

Baroque Collection. Vox/Turnabout PVTS 7601-C (CD); PCTS 7601 (cassette).

Baroque Favorites. Dallas Trumpets. Crystal C-232 (cassette).

Bartok, Bela. *Concerto for Orchestra*. New York Philharmonic Orchestra. Boulez. CBS MK-37259 (CD); MYT-37259 (cassette).

Beethoven, Ludwig van. *Für Elise, Bagatelle Wo056*. Brendel, Piano. Philips 412227-2 PH (CD); 412227-4 PH (cassette).

———. *Sonata no. 8 in C, op. 13, "Pathétique."* Arrau. Philips 420153-2 PH (CD).

———. *Symphony no. 6 in F, op. 68, "Pastorale."* Berlin Philarmonic Orchestra. Karajan. Deutsche Grammophon (Galleria) 415833-2 GGA (CD); 415833-4 GGA (cassette).

Benedictine Monks of the Abbey of St. Maurice and Saint-Maur. *Gregorian Chants*. Philips 432506-2 (CD)

Berg, Alban. *Three Pieces for Orchestra, op. 6*. London Symphony Orchestra. Abbado. Deutsche Grammophon 423238-2 GC (CD).

Best of series. Victrola. Several different recordings featuring a variety of composers.

Beyond Boundaries. (Various artists). Earthbeat Earthb-CD2552 (CD); Earthb-C2552 (cassette).

Billings, William. "Chester," from *Hymns and Fuguing Tunes*. Gregg Smith Singers. Premier Recordings PRCD-1008 (CD).

Brahms, Johannes. *Variations on a Theme by Haydn, op. 56a*. Marlboro Festival Orchestra. Casals. Sony Classical SMK 46247 (CD); SMT 46247 (cassette).

Brubeck, Dave. *Blue Rondo a la Turk*. Concord Jazz CCD 4317 (CD); CJC 317 (cassette).

———. *Unsquare Dance*. Columbia Records SLPX 2177 (LP).

Chieftains. *The Tailor of Gloucester*. Windham Hill/Rabbit Ears Storybook Classics WD-0709 (CD); WT-0709 (cassette).

Chopin, Frédéric. "Étude in E Major," from *Études (24) for Piano, op. 10 and op. 25*. Ashkenazy. London 414127-2LH (CD).

Cooder, Ry. *Pecos Bill*. Windham Hill/Rabbit Ears Storybook Classics WD-0709 (CD); WT-0709 (cassette).

Copland, Aaron. *Appalachian Spring Suite*. Los Angeles Philharmonic Orchestra. Bernstein. Deutsche Grammophon (Leonard Bernstein Edition) 431048-2 GBE (CD); 431048-4 GBE (cassette).

———. *Rodeo*. New York Philharmonic Orchestra. Bernstein. CBS MYK-36727 (CD); MYT-36727 (cassette).

Crumb, George. *Ancient Voices of Children*. Contemporary Chamber Ensemble. Elektra/Nonesuch 79149-2 (CD); N5-71255 (cassette).

Debussy, Claude. "Snowflakes Are Dancing," from *Children's Corner Suite*. Ulster Orchestra. Tortelier. Chandos CHAN-8756 (CD); ABTD-1395 (cassette).

———. "Clair de Lune," from *Suite Bergamasque*. Philadelphia Orchestra. Ormandy. CBS MGT-30950 (cassette).

———. "Syrinx," from *Music of Debussy*. Galway, flute. RCD1-7173 (CD); HREI-7173 (cassette).

Ellington, Duke. "Take the A Train," from *Digital Duke*. GRP Records GRD-9548 (CD).

Gemini. *Rhythmically Moving*. High/Scope Educational Research Foundation M2201-M2209 (CD); M2001C-M2009C (cassette); M2001-M2009 (LP).

Glass, Philip. *Glassworks*. MK-37265 (CD); CBS PMT-37265 (cassette).

Grainger, Percy. *Children's March: Over the Hills and Far Away*. Central Band of the Royal Air Force. EMI Records CDC 7496082 (CD).

Great Baroque Favorites. CBS MYK-38482 (CD); MYT-38482 (cassette).

Greatest Hits series. RCA Victor. Many different recordings featuring various composers and themes.

Grieg, Edvard. *Peer Gynt Suites nos. 1 and 2, op. 46 and op. 55*. Royal Concertgebouw Orchestra. Philips 41158-4 PB (cassette).

Grofé, Ferde. "Sunrise," from *Grand Canyon Suite*. New York Philharmonic Orchestra. Bernstein. CBS MYK-37759 (CD); MYT-37759 (cassette).

Handel, George Frederick. "Le Réjouissance," from *The Royal Fireworks Music*. New York Philharmonic Orchestra. Boulez. CBS MYK-38480 (CD); MYT-38480 (cassette).

———. *Water Music: Suite.* New York Philharmonic Orchestra. Boulez. CBS MYK-38480 (CD); MYT-38480 (cassette).

Hart, Mickey. *Planet Drum.* Rykodisc RYKO-CD10206 (CD); RYKO-C10206 (cassette).

Haydn, Franz Josef. *Symphony no. 94 in G, "Surprise Symphony."* Vienna Philharmonic Orchestra. Bernstein. Deutsche Grammophon 431034-2 GBE (CD); 431034-4 GBE (cassette).

———. *Trios for Piano, Violin and Cello.* Beaux Arts Trio. Philips 422831-2 (CD).

Holst, Gustav. *The Planets, op. 32.* Berlin Philharmonic Orchestra. Karajan. 40028-2 GH (CD); 400028-4 GH (cassette).

Hooked on Classics, vols.1 and 2. K-tel 6051-4 (cassette) 6051-2 (CD). Note: There are several other *Hooked on Classics* titles recorded on K-tel.

Ibert, Jacques. *Trois Pièces Brèves for Wind Quintet.* Tuckwell Quintet. Elektra/Nonesuch 780224 (cassette).

———. *Trois Pièces Brèves for Wind Quintet.* Athena Ensemble. Chandos (Collect) CHAN 6543 (CD).

Instruments. (Various artists). HAN-CD 8302 (CD); HAN-C8302 (cassette).

Isham, Mark. *The Emperor's New Clothes.* Windham Hill/Rabbit Ears Storybook Classics WD-0712 (CD); WT-0717 (cassette).

Italia Mia. The Waverly Consort. CBS MT-36664 (cassette).

Joplin, Scott. *Pine apple Rag.* Albright. MusicMasters 7061-2-C (CD).

———. *"Pine apple Rag,"* from *The Entertainer.* Cornil. Biograph BCD-101 (CD).

Kottke, Leo. *Paul Bunyan.* Windham Hill/Rabbit Ears Storybook Classics WD-0717 (CD); WT-0717 (cassette).

Lande, Art. *The Three Little Pigs.* Windham Hill/Rabbit Ears Storybook Classics WD-0713 (CD); WT-0713 (cassette).

Lully, Jean Baptiste. *Marches and Field Music: Music of the Baroque and Classical Periods.* Calig CAL 50844 (CD).

MacDowell, Edward. *Woodland Sketches for Piano, op. 51.* Fierro, piano. Elektra/Nonesuch 71411-4 (cassette).

Masterpieces of Music before 1750: An Anthology of Music, vol. 1: Gregorian Chant to J. S. Bach. Haydn Society Records CD-7-9038 (CD).

McFerrin, Bobby. *The Elephant's Child.* Windham Hill/Rabbit Ears Storybook Classics WD-0701 (CD); WT-0701 (cassette).

Mozart, Wolfgang Amadeus. "Marriage of Figaro" overture, from *The Mozart Collection.* London Sinfonietta. Rutter. American Gramophone AGCD-586 (CD); AGC-586 (cassette).

———. "Marriage of Figaro" overture, from *Mozart Weekend.* London Weekend Classics 425513-2 LC (CD).

———. *Serenade no. 10 in B-flat Major, K.361.* Orchestra of the 18th Century. Barenboim. Philips 422338-2PH (CD); 422338-4PH (cassette).

———. *Serenade no. 13 in G, K.525, "Eine Kleine Nachtmusik,"* from *Compact Mozart.* Sony Classical 5 SBK 45977 (CD).

———. *Serenade no. 13 in G, K.525, "Eine Kleine Nachtmusik,"* Vienna Mozart Ensemble. Boskovsky. London 425874-2 LC (CD); 411846-4 LT (cassette).

————. "Minuet," from *Symphony no. 40 in G, K.550*. London Symphony Orchestra. Abbado. Deutsche Grammophon (Galleria) 415841-2 GGA (CD).

————. "Minuet," from *Symphony no. 40 in G, K.550*. Vienna Philharmonic Orchestra (Leonard Bernstein Edition) Deutsche Grammophon 431040-2 GBE (CD); 431040-4 GBE (cassette).

————. *Variations on "Ah! Vous dirai-je maman," K.265*. Eschenbach. Deutsche Grammophon 429808-2 GMM (CD); 429808-4GMM (cassette).

Paganini, Niccolo. *Moto Perpetuo, op. 11*. NBC Symphony. Toscanini. Dell'Arte DA9020 (CD).

Penderecki, Krystoff. *Threnody for the Victims of Hiroshima*. Polish Radio and TV Symphony. Kawalla. Conifer CDCF-168 (CD); MCFC-168 (cassette).

Poulenc, Francis. *Sonata for Flute and Piano*. Rampal. Odyssey YT-33905 (cassette).

————. *Sonata for Flute and Piano*. Snowden. Virgin Classics VC790846-2 (CD); VC790846-4 (cassette).

Putmayo Presents: The Best of World Music, vol. 1: World Vocal. Rhino Rhino-CD 71203 (CD); Rhino-C71203 (cassette).

Putmayo Presents: The Best of World Music, vol. 2: Instrumental Music. Rhino RhinoCD 71204 (CD); C71204 (cassette).

Rachmaninoff, Sergei. *Vocalise, op. 34, no. 14*. Scottish National Orchestra. Murphey. Chandos CHAN-8476 (CD); ABTD-1187 (cassette).

Royal Brass: Music from the Renaissance and Baroque. Empire Brass. Telarc CD-80257 (CD); CS-30301 (cassette).

Rutter, John. *The Reluctant Dragon*. Masterchord MCK412 (cassette).

————. *The Wind in the Willows*. Masterchord MCK412 (cassette).

Schoenberg, Arnold. *Pierrot Lunaire, op. 21*. Contemporary Chamber Ensemble, Weisberg. Elektra/Nonesuch 71251 (cassette).

————. *Pierrot Lunaire, op. 21*. Nash Ensemble, Rattle. Chandos ABR-1046 (CD).

Schola Antiqua. (Gregorian Chants). L'Oiseau-Lyre 425114-2 (CD).

Schubert, Franz. "The Trout," from *Quintet in A for Piano and Strings, D. 667*. Budapest String Quartet. Sony Classical (Essential Classics) SBK-46343 (CD); SBT-46343 (cassette).

————. *Symphony no. 8 in B, D. 759, "Unfinished."* Berlin Philharmonic Orchestra. Barenboim. CBS MK-39676 (CD); 1MT-39676 (cassette).

Sibelius, Jean. *Symphony no. 2 in D, op. 43*. New York Philharmonic Orchestra. Bernstein. CBS MYK-38477 (CD); MYT-38477 (cassette).

Smetna, Bedrich. *The Moldau*. Chicago Symphony. Barenboim. Deutsche Grammophon (Galleria) 415851-2 GGA (CD); 415851-4 GGA (cassette).

Solid Gold Baroque. "Winter" (Vivaldi). Vanguard Classics OVC 4021-CED.

Sousa, John Philip. *Band of the Grenadier Guards*. London Weekend Classics 430211-2 LC (CD); 430211-4 LC (cassette).

Story, Tim. *The Legend of Sleepy Hollow*. Windham Hill/Rabbit Ears Storybook Classics WD-0711 (CD); WT-0711 (cassette).

Stravinsky, Igor. *Ebony Concerto for Clarinet and Jazz Ensemble*. Goodman. CBS MK-42227 (CD); MT-42227 (cassette).

————. *Fanfare for a New Theatre for Two Trumpets*. London Sinfonietta. Chailly. London 417114-2LH (CD).

———. "Dance of the Adolescents," from *The Rite of Spring*. Boston Symphony. Monteux. RCA (Papillion Collection) 6529-2-R6 (CD); 6529-4-RC (cassette).

———. *Suites nos. 1 and 2 for Small Orchestra*. London Sinfonietta. Chailly. London 417114-2LH (CD).

Susato, Tielman. *Hits of 1500*. Augsburg Early Music Ensemble. Christophous CD-74572 (CD).

Taj Mahal. *Brer Rabbit and the Wonderful Tar Baby*. Windham Hill/Rabbit Ears Storybook Classics WD-0716 (CD); WT-0716 (cassette).

Tchaikovsky, Piotr Ilyich. "Dance of the Toy Flutes," from *The Nutcracker Suite, op. 71A*. Suisse Romande. Ansermet. London 417097-4LT (cassette).

———. "Dance of the Toy Flutes," from *The Nutcracker Suite, op. 71A*. New York Philharmonic Orchestra. Bernstein. CBS MYK-37238 (CD); MYT-37238 (cassette).

Telemann, Georg Philipp. "Réjouissance," from *Suite in A for Flute and Strings*. Madeira Festival Orchestra. Newman. Vox/Turnabout PVT 7185 (CD); PCT 7185 (cassette).

Treasury of Early Music, vol. 1. (Gregorian Chants). Haydn Society Records 79038 (CD).

Treasury of Early Music, vol. 2. VO13 Haydn Society Records CD-7 9101 (CD).

Varèse, Edgar. *Poème Electronique*. Neuma 450-74 (CD).

Vaughn Williams, Ralph. *English Folk Song Suite*. London Wind Orchestra. Wick. Elektra/Nonesuch N1-78002 (cassette).

Vivaldi, Antonio. *The Four Seasons, op. 8, nos. 1-4*. I Musici. Agostini. Philips 426847-2 PH (CD); 426847-4 PH (cassette).

———. "Winter," from *Solid Gold Baroque*. Vanguard Classics OVC 4021-CED.

Vollenweider, Andreas. *Down to the Moon*. CBS MK-4225 (CD); FMT-4255 (cassette).

United Artists of Messidor. Messidor MESSI-CD 15823 (CD).

Wagner, Richard. "Ride of the Valkyries," from *Der Ring des Nibelungen*. New York Philharmonic Orchestra. Mehta. CBS MDK-44657 (CD); MDT-44657 (cassette).

Webern, Anton. *Five Pieces for Orchestra, op. 10*. London Symphony Orchestra. Dorati. Mercury (Living Presence) 432006-2 (CD).

Winston, George. *The Velveteen Rabbit*. Dancing Cat DCD-3007 (CD); DCT-3007 (cassette).

World Beat Explosion. (Various artists). SHAN-C64008 (cassette).

World Music Sampler. (Various artists). SHAN-CD9101 (CD); SHAN-C9101 (cassette).

World Music Sampler. Lyrichord World Music. LYRCD-7414 (CD).

Appendix

SOURCES FOR
INSTRUMENTS, BOOKS, AND RECORDINGS

Anyone Can Whistle (unique assortment of musical instruments, books, and recordings). P.O. Box 4407, Kingston, NY 12401.

August House (extensive storytelling publications). P.O. Box 3223, Little Rock, AR 72203. (800) 284-8784.

Backyard Music (cardboard dulcimer kits and instruments). David Cross, P.O. Box 9047, New Haven, CT 06532. (203) 469-5756.

Classics (collections of music of all styles and types). Minnesota Communications Group, P.O. Box 64502, St. Paul, MN 55164-0502.

Dover Publications, Inc. (extensive book lists; catalogs of general and children's music books). 31 East 2nd St., Mineola, NY 11501.

Elderly Instruments (instruments, books, recordings). 1100 N. Washington, P.O. Box 14210, Lansing, MI 48901. (517) 372-7890.

Folk Beat Percussion (ethnic percussion instruments). 509 E. 10th St., Newport, KY 41071. (800) 228-2328.

Friendship House (music gifts, posters, books, games, recordings, and tapes, including Music of Man video series by Yehudi Menuhin). 29313 Clemens Rd. #2G, P.O. Box 450978, Cleveland, OH 44145-0623. (216) 871-8040.

General Music Store (classroom instruments, books, recordings). 19880 State Line Rd., South Bend, IN 46637. (800) 348-5003.

Music for Little People (instruments, games, music, recordings, and books for children). P.O. Box 1460, Redway, CA 95560.

Music Is Elementary (classroom instruments, books). P.O. Box 24263, Cleveland, OH 44124. (800) 888-7502.

National Storytelling Association. P.O. Box 309, Jonesborough, TN 37659-9983. (800) 525-4514. This is a professional organization for storytellers. A membership includes the bimonthly *Storytelling Magazine*, a bimonthly newsletter, and reduced rates for NSA events. NSA sponsors the National Storytelling Festival (in October) and the National Storytelling Conference (in July). Catalog of books and tapes.

Olive Press (multicultural books and teaching resources). 5727 Dunmore, West Bloomfield, MI 48322. (810) 855-6063.

Rhythm Band, Inc. (classroom instruments and books). P.O. Box 126, Ft. Worth, TX 761010126. (800) 424-4724.

Signals (recordings of all styles). WGBH Educational Foundation, P.O. Box 64428, St. Paul, MN 55164-0428.

Sound Exchange (wide variety of classical, jazz, pop, world music, and new age recordings). 45 N. Industry Ct., Deer Park, NY 11729. (800) 521-0042.

Ward Brodt Music Mall (music supplies and books). 2200 W. Beltline Highway, P.O. Box 526, Madison, WI 53701. (800) 369-6255.

West Music Company (classroom instruments, music, and books). P.O. Box 5521, 1212 5th St., Coralville, IA 52241. (800) 397-9378.

Windham Hill Records (recordings). P.O. Box 9388, Stanford, CA 94309. (415) 329-0647.

Wireless (good selections of popular classics, folk, world, jazz, popular, and new age music). Minnesota Public Radio, P.O. Box 64422, St. Paul, MN 55164-0422. (800) 669-9999.

World of Peripole (preschool music instruments and supplies). Browns Mills, NJ 08015. (609) 893-9111.

Glossary

LITERARY ELEMENTS

plot. The sequence of events in a story; not only *what* happens, but *in what order*; includes the relationship between events and conflict.

character. A person, animal, or creature featured in a story; the *who* of a story.

setting. The place and time period of a story; the *where* and *when* of a story; may also include weather, and the political and social background of the time.

theme. The meaningful concepts of a story; the central or dominant idea that transcends a story by application to the reader's world; the *why* of a story, made concrete by details and emphasis.

point of view. The angle from which a story's events are viewed and told; the most common are third person (uses the words *he, she, it*) and first person (uses the word *I*); the point of view affects a story's meaning.

style. An author's use of language, particularly patterns of word choice, syntax, imagery, figures of speech, and plain or elaborate structures, to create a distinctive narrative style.

tone. The attitude of the speaker or author toward the story's subject or theme, determined from a story's content and style (for example, tone may be described as "light-hearted," "somber," or "ironic").

GENERAL LITERARY TERMS

improvisational drama. Drama that is invented on the spot by an actor in response to a situation or another character; drama that is not based on a script, nor on an actor's pre-formed ideas.

literary folktale. An authored story in a folklore style; folktales with a known author; writers often draw upon traditional characters and motifs in these stories.

narrative (imaginative) fiction. Short or novel-length stories that are the product of a writer's imagination; can include real people or events, but the plot itself is the writer's invention.

oral tradition. The prehistoric practice of storytelling; various types of narratives have developed out of storytelling, such as myths, epics, and legends; stories in this tradition do not have a "known" author.

persona. Literally, "mask"; describes the self (created by the author) in the telling of a story; a story's narrative voice.

readers theatre. A dramatic presentation in which participants read their parts from a prepared script, without costumes or staging (particularly suitable for classrooms).

story theatre. A type of drama in which characters perform in mime, or with minimal dialogue, as a narrator tells the story either from a prepared script or from memory; can be presented without staging, or it can be fully staged with costumes, scenery, and lighting.

MUSIC TERMS

absolute music. Music that is free from nonmusical implications.

aesthetics. The study of that which makes up a work of art.

atonal. Twentieth-century music that rejects the framework of musical key.

body percussion. Rhythmic patterns created from sounds using the body (feet, hands, fingers, toes, chest, etc.).

brass instrument. Any instrument that creates sounds when air is vibrated through the lips and amplified through a mouthpiece and the instrument itself.

classical music. Music that embraces the form, structure, and balance of the work of a composer; a more proper term is "art" music.

composer. A person who organizes sounds into musical works.

consonance. Introduces into music the relaxation and fulfillment of sound through harmony.

dissonance. Introduces into music necessary tension through harmony; dissonance is to music what suspense and conflict are to drama.

dynamics. Different degrees of aural volume.

embouchure. The proper position of the lips for playing wind instruments.

folk music. Music representing a tradition of a community that is usually transmitted aurally.

found sounds. Any sounds in the immediate environment that are available for use in sound compositions.

glockenspiel. A percussion instrument consisting of a set of barred bells.

guiro. A scraping instrument, usually in the shape of a fish, popular in South American countries.

harmony. The vertical, or chordal, structure of music.

homophonic. Music texture consisting of one melodic line and harmonic accompaniment.

improvisation. The art of performing music spontaneously.

medieval music. Music created during the years A.D. 500 to 1450.

melody. A succession of musical tones that represent the horizontal element of music.

monophonic. A single-voice or single-melody texture without accompaniment.

music. In its simplest definition, "organized sounds."

musique concrete. Music created from recorded sounds of various sources.

orchestration. The art of employing various instrumental sounds in a musical composition.

percussion. Instruments that create sounds when hit, shaken, beaten, or rubbed.

pitch. The location of a musical sound in the tonal scale.

polyphonic. When two or more melodic lines are combined to create a many-voiced texture.

program music. Music inspired by a nonmusical idea that can "tell a story."

renaissance music. Music created during the years A.D. 1450 to 1600 that displays the general traits of classical music.

rhythm. The feeling of "movement" in music.

rondo. A musical structure that has a (repeating) passage after each section, usually represented ABACADA.

string instrument. Any instrument with strings that create sounds when plucked or bowed.

tempo. The speed of a piece of music.

texture. The method in which lines of music make up a musical "fabric."

timbre. The quality, or "color," of a tone.

tone. A sound of definite pitch and duration.

woodwind instrument. Any instrument with an enclosed "column" that creates sounds when air is blown through the column.

xylophone. A percussion instrument consisting of graduated wooden bars, which are struck to create sounds.

Activity Age Index

About the Authors

Dr. Barbara Britsch has been a professional storyteller for fourteen years, locally (in Ohio) and nationally. Her storytelling in schools involves children in telling, writing, and illustrating their own stories. As an assistant professor of literature and writing at Lourdes College in Sylvania, Ohio, one of her prime areas of interest and study is teaching literature for children, one of the many ways of exploring literature in the classroom. She has conducted numerous teacher workshops on this subject and is currently a member of the Storytelling Committee of the National Council of Teachers of English.

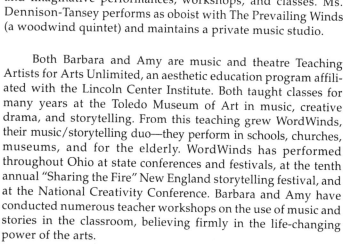

Amy Dennison-Tansey has been involved in creative music education since 1980, including ten years at the Toledo Museum of Art. She holds a degree in music education and a master's degree in music as a woodwind specialist. Ms. Dennison-Tansey has worked with the education programs at the Children's Museum of Cincinnati and the Contemporary Arts Center of Cincinnati, and in school districts, bookstores, summer camps, and other venues. Her goal of making music accessible to all ages and abilities is achieved through interactive and imaginative performances, workshops, and classes. Ms. Dennison-Tansey performs as oboist with The Prevailing Winds (a woodwind quintet) and maintains a private music studio.

Both Barbara and Amy are music and theatre Teaching Artists for Arts Unlimited, an aesthetic education program affiliated with the Lincoln Center Institute. Both taught classes for many years at the Toledo Museum of Art in music, creative drama, and storytelling. From this teaching grew WordWinds, their music/storytelling duo—they perform in schools, churches, museums, and for the elderly. WordWinds has performed throughout Ohio at state conferences and festivals, at the tenth annual "Sharing the Fire" New England storytelling festival, and at the National Creativity Conference. Barbara and Amy have conducted numerous teacher workshops on the use of music and stories in the classroom, believing firmly in the life-changing power of the arts.